Spiritual Masters: East and West
Series

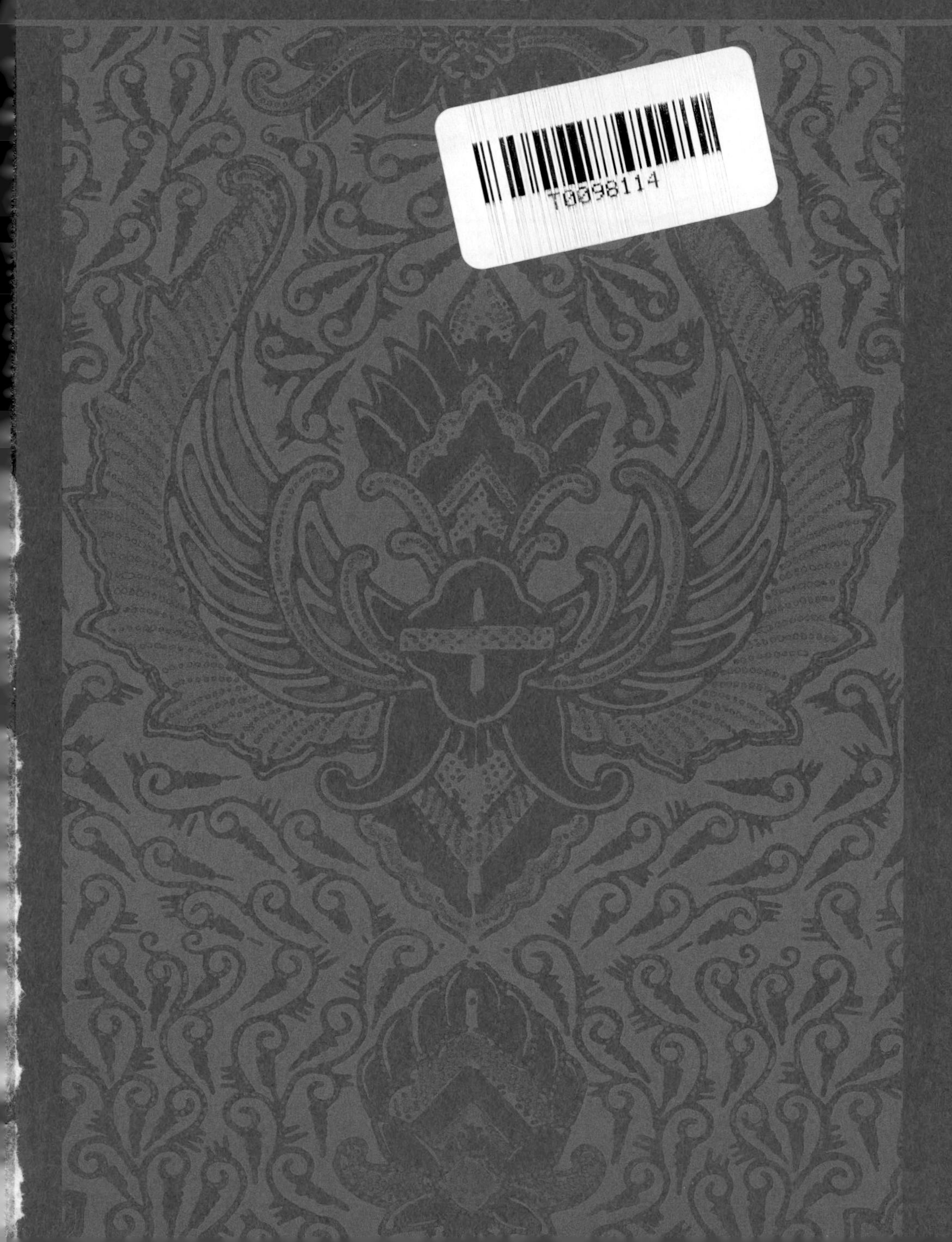

About This Book

"Without an understanding of Hōnen it is not possible to get to the essence of the Pure Land Way, much less to walk it. World Wisdom has provided a priceless service to contemporary Pure Land Buddhists in making him and his teaching accessible to a wider readership. The Buddhist world will ever be grateful to them."

—**Jim Pym**, Pure Land Buddhist Fellowship, U.K.

"The first significant English publication on Hōnen and his teachings."

—**Hirokawa Takatoshi**, Taisho University, Tokyo, and translator of *Hōnen's Senchakushu: Passages on the Selection of the Nembutsu in the Original Vow*

"Hōnen stands as a giant among religious reformers…. It really is a remarkable achievement to have edited [*Honen the Buddhist Saint*] down to a readable form."

—**Clark Strand**, author of *Seeds from a Birch Tree: Writing Haiku and the Spiritual Journey*

"Hōnen was a pioneer…. In our present day, it is important to rekindle the spirit that motivated him and his critical insight and attitude to society, if the ordinary person is to find meaning and hope in the desolate wasteland of modern, secular society."

—**Alfred Bloom**, University of Hawaii, and author of *Shinran's Gospel of Pure Grace*

"A truly remarkable translation of a classic biography of Saint Hōnen … a pivotal figure of the late Heian and early Kamakura Periods. Most fortunately, Joseph Fitzgerald has prepared a shortened version, through skillful editing and adaptation…. There is little doubt that this abridgement will serve to open doors ever wider, guiding all who come upon it into the life and thought of that extraordinary Pure Land priest Saint Hōnen and ultimately into the very heart of the Amida Buddha Himself."

—**Rev. Tetsuo Unno**, Shin Buddhist minister, Buddhist Churches of America

"From the fifteen hundred years of the intellectual history of Japanese Buddhism, if I were to choose one thinker, it would have to be Hōnen."

—**Kato Shuichi**, Ritsumeikan University, Kyoto, and author of *Japan: Spirit & Form*

World Wisdom

The Library of Perennial Philosophy

The Library of Perennial Philosophy is dedicated to the exposition of the timeless Truth underlying the diverse religions. This Truth, often referred to as the *Sophia Perennis*—or Perennial Wisdom—finds its expression in the revealed Scriptures as well as the writings of the great sages and the artistic creations of the traditional worlds.

Honen the Buddhist Saint: Essential Writings and Official Biography appears as one of our selections in the Spiritual Masters: East & West series.

Spiritual Masters: East & West Series

This series presents the writings of great spiritual masters of the past and present from both East and West. Carefully selected essential writings of these sages are combined with biographical information, glossaries of technical terms, historical maps, and pictorial and photographic art in order to communicate a sense of their respective spiritual climates.

Hōnen Shōnin

Honen the Buddhist Saint

Essential Writings and Official Biography

From the 14th Century Manuscript
Compiled by Imperial Order

Edited and Adapted by
JOSEPH A. FITZGERALD

Foreword by
CLARK STRAND

Introduction by
ALFRED BLOOM

Translation by
REV. HARPER HAVELOCK COATES &
REV. RYUGAKU ISHIZUKA

Library of Congress Cataloging-in-Publication Data

Honen Shonin eden. English.
Honen the Buddhist saint : essential writings and official biography from the 14th century manuscript compiled by imperial order / edited and adapted by Joseph A. Fitzgerald ; foreword by Clark Strand ; introduction by Alfred Bloom ; translation by Harper Havelock Coates & Ryugaku Ishizuka.
p. cm. -- (Spiritual masters: East and West series)
Includes index.
ISBN-13: 978-1-933316-13-0 (pbk. : alk. paper)
ISBN-10: 1-933316-13-6 (pbk. : alk. paper) 1. Honen, 1133-1212. 2. Jodoshu--Doctrines--Early works to 1800. 3. Priests, Jodoshu--Japan--Biography--Early works to 1800. I. Fitzgerald, Joseph A., 1977- II. Strand, Clark, 1957- III. Bloom, Alfred. IV. Coates, Harper Havelock, 1865- V. Ishizuka, Ryugaku. VI. Title. VII. Series.
BQ8649.H667H63713 2006
294.3'926--dc22
[B]

2006016570

Cover art: "The Halo Bridge"

Printed on acid-free paper in Canada.

For information address World Wisdom, Inc.
P.O. Box 2682, Bloomington, Indiana 47402-2682

www.worldwisdom.com

CONTENTS

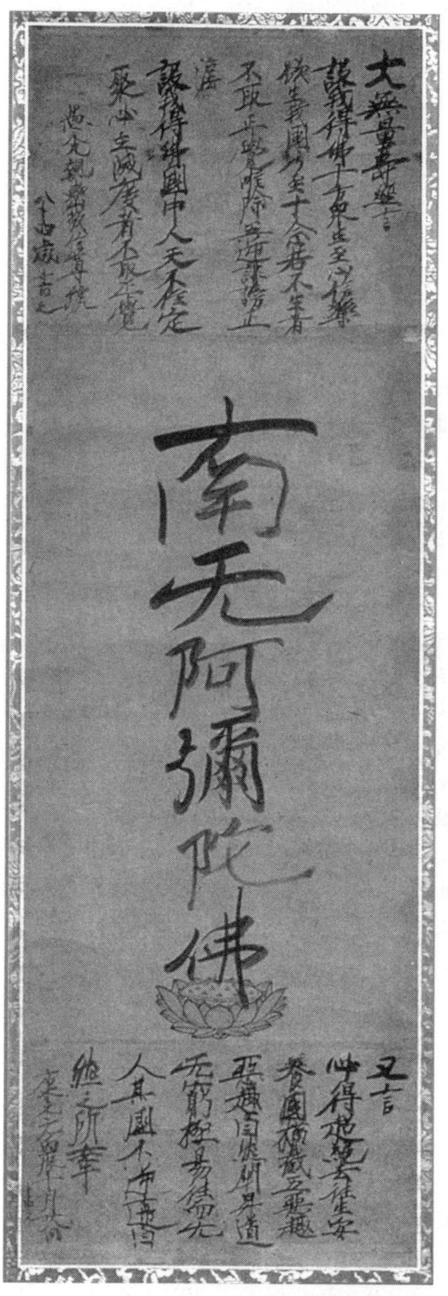

Namu Amida Butsu
Calligraphy by Shinran Shōnin

FOREWORD

"Know that you do not know," said Socrates, "and that is knowledge." With that ancient but very simple teaching in mind, it is easy to understand why the founders of Japanese Pure Land Buddhism adopted names for themselves such as Guchi no Hōnen-bo ("Hōnen the Foolish") or Gutoku Shinran ("Stubble-headed Shinran"), and the reason why, when asked about the value of intellectual learning on the Pure Land path, Hōnen once remarked, "The moment a scholar is born, he forgets the *Nembutsu*."

Despite his mild manner as a person and the fact that his teachings are, finally, so simple that they can be grasped in their entirety even by an illiterate person, Hōnen stands as a giant among religious reformers. Before him no Buddhist teacher in Japan or elsewhere had ever dared to advance the teaching that all are saved by the miraculous power of the Tathāgata, regardless of whether they are young or old, rich or poor, male or female, foolish or wise. Always some form of monastic training or practice was required, or one had to be wealthy enough to acquire karmic merit in some other way, by building temples or supporting monks, for instance. This set the Buddha way far beyond the reach of ordinary men and women struggling in the world. Especially disenfranchised were those who engaged in occupations such as hunting or fishing—traditionally regarded by Buddhists as evil or karmically defiled—and women, whose spiritual salvation was often believed to depend upon their being reborn as men. Hōnen was the first Buddhist teacher to include such people in his vision of spiritual salvation. For this alone he deserves the title appended to his name by the translators of this volume. He was, indeed, a saint.

Today Hōnen is known as the founder of the Jōdo or "Pure Land" school of Japanese Buddhism, but I believe it would be a mistake to suppose that Hōnen simply read the Pure Land Sūtras and took them to heart. Hōnen followed a long tradition of great Pure Land teachers in India, China, and Japan, but none of his predecessors embodied the teachings to the extent that Hōnen did, welcoming women, farmers, tradesmen, and even lepers into his community. Because of his deep humility and his compassion for the disenfranchised, Hōnen took the idea of universal salvation profoundly to heart and reinterpreted the Pure Land teachings to fit that vision. The

The Buddha Amida

result was a tradition which culminated in what the scholar D. T. Suzuki considered the most remarkable development of Mahāyāna Buddhism ever achieved in East Asia.

I first encountered Hōnen through a document called the *Ichimai Kishōmon*, or "One-Page Testament," a summary of the Pure Land teaching offered by Hōnen to the disciple who attended him at his deathbed. Years later it remains in my mind the touchstone of simplicity and spiritual sincerity against which I measure everything I write. In it, Hōnen presents his doctrine of salvation through single-hearted recitation of the name of Amida Buddha in the simplest possible terms, after which he adds:

> Those who believe this, though they clearly understand all the teachings Shaka [Shākyamuni] taught throughout his whole life, should behave themselves like simple-minded folk, who know not a single letter, or like ignorant nuns or monks whose faith is implicitly simple. Thus without pedantic airs, they should fervently practice the repetition of the name of Amida, and that alone.

To the document itself, Hōnen then affixes the imprint of his palms, by way of authentication, and concludes: "I, Hōnen, have no other teaching than this. In order to prevent misinterpretation after my passing away, I make this final testament."

It is extremely moving to see Hōnen's hands superimposed over the text of this document. It affects me in the way that I imagine many Catholics or Orthodox Christians must feel in the presence of holy relics. But it is also more than that, because I don't believe that Hōnen's handprints, or the paper they are imprinted on, have any special power in themselves. For me the power lies in the fact that they express the essence of all religion. They seem to say, "This is the truth I lived for . . . and the truth I lived."

Clark Strand

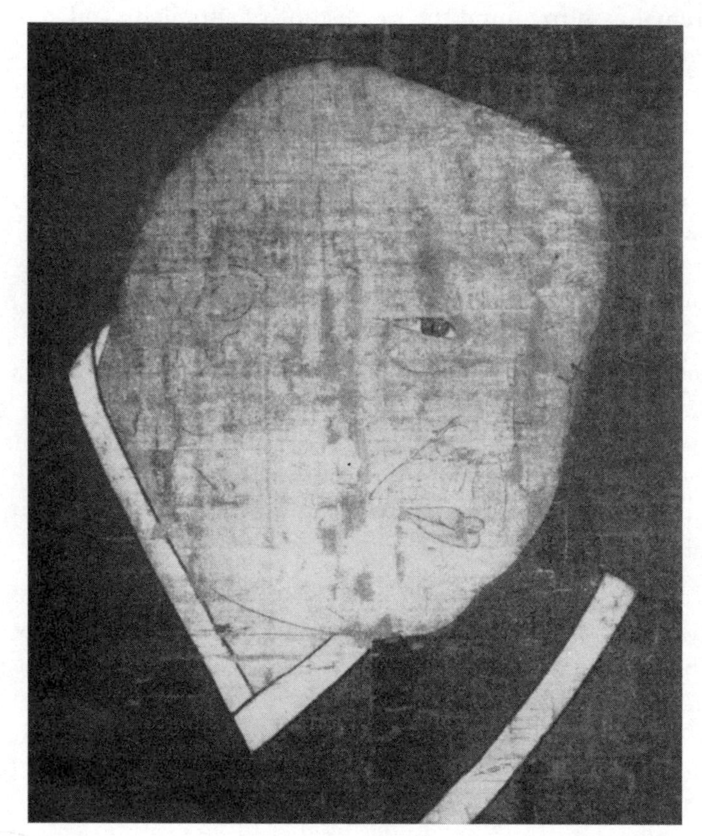

Hōnen Shōnin

PREFACE

Namu Amida Butsu
"Save me, oh! Amida Buddha"[1]

Hōnen's own handwritten copy of the *Nembutsu*

For the twelfth century saint, Hōnen Shōnin, founder of the many-branched Jōdo ("Pure Land") school of Buddhism in Japan, this is the all-in-all of spiritual salvation.

> Only repeat the name of Amida with all your heart. Whether walking or standing, sitting or lying, never cease the practice of it even for a moment. This is the very work which unfailingly issues in salvation, for it is in accordance with the Original Vow of that Buddha. (Hōnen, quoting Zendō [Chinese: Shan-tao])

Hōnen paid respect to the forms of Buddhism that existed in his day, and he recognized antecedents to his views, most notably the great Chinese Pure Land teacher Zendō, but fundamentally his message was a departure, a new beginning. According to Hōnen, the old ways and forms of Buddhism are legitimate—as each relates to the teachings of the historical Buddha, Shākyamuni—but they pertain to a golden age that is no more. We live, to quote a recurring phrase of Hōnen's, in "these latter degenerate days," when man is no longer up to the discipline and teachings of past doctrines.

The answer for mankind today, Hōnen teaches, is the practice of the *Nembutsu*—the repetition of *Namu Amida Butsu*, accompanied by faith in the saving power of Amida's name. For Amida Buddha made a vow, which he fulfilled innumerable ages ago, that each person who calls upon his name with faith but ten times, or even once, shall be born

[1] This is the Coates-Ishizuka translation. Alternate translations include: "I entrust myself to Amida Buddha"; "Praise to the Buddha Amida"; and "I take refuge in Amida Buddha."

into his Pure Land of Bliss. The practice of *Nembutsu* is simplicity itself; it requires neither proficiency, nor intelligence, nor virtue (though it does not reject any of these things); it requires only repetition and faith, faith in the saving power of the vow that Amida Buddha made. "Here we surely have something just suited to our several capacities, have we not?" (Hōnen)

Amida made his vow and attained Enlightenment eons before the life of the historical Buddha, Shākyamuni, but it is thanks to Shaka (as the Japanese call Shākyamuni) that Amida's name shall be remembered for all time: "Preserve well these words," Shaka said to Ānanda, his favorite disciple. "I mean preserve well the name of the Buddha of Endless Life [Amitāyus, a term for Amida]." Here one enlightened being (Shaka) preserves for posterity the memory of an earlier enlightened being (Amida).[2] Hōnen, though he would have certainly rejected the comparison, likewise has helped to preserve the name of Amida. So beautiful and so simple, his words on Amida have been heard by millions, and Amida's name has been on their lips because of him.

At the level of faith there is no difference between a common-born man and a noble-born man; the path Hōnen preaches is for the two equally. Someone once suggested to Hōnen that his practice of the *Nembutsu* was better than the *Nembutsu* practice of a man who was his attendant. With evident anger Hōnen responded, "Well, to what purpose have you all along been listening to the doctrine of the Pure Land? That Awanosuke [his attendant] over there, when he asks the Buddha to save him, saying, '*Namu Amida Butsu*,' does just the same as I do when I offer that petition. There is not the slightest difference between us."

Hōnen's openness toward the common man, and his drastic simplification of religious doctrine and practice, was a departure from the priest-centered, doctrinally-oriented Buddhism of the day. Hōnen was himself a priest, from fifteen years of age until the day he died, and never in all that time did he disparage the institution of the priesthood. There were, nevertheless, priests and scholars of the established Buddhist sects who watched Hōnen with a wary and concerned eye, for they believed the rapid "ten-

[2] For an explanation of the perhaps surprising preeminence of Amida over the historical Buddha, see Frithjof Schuon's article, "Dharmakara's Vow" published in *Treasures of Buddhism* (Bloomington, IN: World Wisdom Books, 1993), pp. 153-165.

thousand fold" spread of his *Nembutsu* doctrine threatened to overwhelm their distinctive traditions. Eventually concern led to persecution, and persecution led to exile by order of the Emperor, when Hōnen was already an old man. His response was characteristic:

> I have labored here in the capital these many years for the spread of the *Nembutsu*, and so I have long wished to get away into the country to preach to those on field and plain, but the time never came for the fulfillment of my wish. Now, however, by the august favor of His Majesty, circumstances have combined to enable me to do so.

After several years of exile, Hōnen was pardoned, thanks to the intercession of admirers in the uppermost ranks of society. He returned to the capital city just in time to die there, and by death attain *Ōjō*, or birth into Amida's Pure Land. He died, in the year 1212 A.D., at the ripe and auspicious age of eighty, the same age at which Shākyamuni left life in the body.

The influence of a great man often increases with death. Since the death of Hōnen Shōnin, nearly eight hundred years ago, it is not an exaggeration to say that countless millions of souls have been touched at a profound level by his words and deeds. Eighty years ago when this book was first published, the translators chose to inform their readers that there were in the order of sixteen million Japanese practitioners of the Jōdo faith, including its many sub-sects.[3] Today, as calculated by Japan's Ministry of Education, the number of practitioners approaches twenty million. One can—and we believe should—be inspired by the teachings of Hōnen, but if nothing else one should be intrigued to learn more about a man whose message has meant so much to so many.

The work that follows relates both the life-story and essential teaching of Hōnen. It was compiled within a century after Hōnen's death, by order of the retired Emperor Go-Fushimi, and was first made available to the English speaking world in 1925 when, after 1030 hours of effort expended over the course of seventeen years, the Reverends Harper H. Coates and Ryugaku Ishizuka finished their translation of the work and published it as *Honen the Buddhist Saint: His Life and Teaching*. It is the only biography of Hōnen ever to have been translated into English.

[3] The largest sect, by far, is the Jōdo Shin Shū, discussed further below. Other sects are not as large, but still thrive. Of the Jōdo sects, the Jōdo Shū is the most closely aligned with the personage and teachings of Hōnen, and claims, therefore, to be the most orthodox.

Surprisingly little has been written in English on Hōnen. As Professor Soga Ryōjin has aptly noted, Hōnen and his form of Pure Land Buddhism "is undeservedly still almost a terra incognita."[4] Aside from a smattering of articles spread across academic journals or embedded in anthologies, *Honen the Buddhist Saint* is one of only a handful of English language books devoted to the presentation of Hōnen's life and message. The lack of available material is made even more puzzling by the fact that one of Hōnen's disciples, Shinran,[5] and the Jōdo sect that he founded (the Jōdo Shin Shū) has received so much attention. Libraries are chock full of books on "Shin Buddhism," as Shinran's Jōdo sect is generally called in the West ("Shin" simply means "true"). Yet the founding father of Jōdo in Japan—the first light, so to speak[6]—is almost unknown[7] and certainly under-appreciated outside his home country. It is a shame, and it is our hope that the present essentialized rendering of Hōnen's official biography will add to the West's understanding of who he was and what he stood for. It is also our belief that as one of the world's most moving and affecting expositors of the power of Faith, the spread of Hōnen's words cannot but contribute to the spiritual betterment of mankind.

Editorial Goals & Methods

As it first appeared in 1925, *Honen the Buddhist Saint* was, by any standard, a massive work. The original fourteenth century biography is already

[4] Frederick Franck, ed., *The Buddha Eye: An Anthology of the Kyoto School and Its Contemporaries* (Bloomington, IN: World Wisdom, Inc, 2004), p. 230.

[5] Shinran's indebtedness to Hōnen (and faith in the *Nembutsu*) is such that he could say: "I would not regret even if I were deceived by Hōnen and thus, by uttering the *Nembutsu* fell into hell. . . . Since I am incapable of any practice whatsoever, hell would definitely be my dwelling anyway" (from Inagaki Hisao's translation of Shinran's *Tannishō*, Chapter II, quoted by Marco Pallis in *A Buddhist Spectrum: Contributions to Buddhist-Christian Dialogue* [Bloomington, IN: World Wisdom, Inc, 2002], p. 121).

[6] Just as Shankara was not the first to discuss the Vedānta, so Hōnen was not the first to discuss the Pure Land: there was a Pure Land school in China from at least the fifth century A.D., and in Japan as well the Pure Land was known. It was Hōnen, however, who added intensity, urgency, and uniqueness to the Pure Land path: what before had been mere seeds or starts burst into bloom, as he brought focus and clarity to nascent teachings, and as he pruned away all extraneous practices in order to focus on what he saw as the "one thing needful," the recitation of the *Nembutsu* that is in accord with Amida's Original Vow.

[7] Notwithstanding, Hōnen was known to figures as diverse as Alan Watts, Joseph Campbell, Martin Heidegger, and Jack Kerouac, in addition, of course, to specialists of Japanese history, among them the well known and respected D.T. Suzuki.

a lengthy work, and to it the translators added approximately 150 pages of introductory material, at least 250 pages of explanatory endnotes, and 190 pages worth of table of contents, index, and lists of Chinese characters. The most common printing available in libraries in the United States is a five volume set, with most of the individual volumes exceeding the thickness of the present book. The goal of the translators was to produce nothing less than "a thesaurus of Japanese Buddhism." In this they proved in some ways successful—their introduction and notes cover vast swaths of political, social, economic, and religious history—but at the price of readability. To read the original book cover-to-cover is an experience akin to a marathon, a task fit only for the specialist academic. Our goal, therefore, was to present the biography of Hōnen—the only one thus far translated into English—in a format, and at a length, that make it accessible to the general student of religion. Everything is maintained that is essential to the story of Hōnen's life and of the description of his teaching. We have changed the order and titling of passages and we have reduced or eliminated certain passages.[8] We have also eliminated many of the original translators' notes, but have kept those that were required for a basic understanding of the text. Many of the notes have been shortened; a handful are new to the current edition. This edition also includes a new glossary. By allowing the reader more easily, quickly, and enjoyably to navigate through *Honen the Buddhist Saint*, we intended to give new life to a worthy but daunting text. Hōnen was a man who spoke to all people, to the religious specialist and to the fisherman. May it be possible for Hōnen to speak once again to those high or low—to anyone who wishes to hear of his path for salvation.

JOSEPH A. FITZGERALD

[8] In order to enhance readability we have presented the text as a continuous narrative, without interrupting its flow with notations of our deletions or rearrangements; in addition, a handful of words have been added for clarification or in order to weave shifted passages into the flow of the text. Readers interested primarily in a scholarly study of Hōnen are urged to consult the unabridged original.

The Nishi Hongwanji, the main seat of the Jōdo Shin sect, founded by Shinran Shōnin

INTRODUCTION

Pure Land Buddhism is becoming more widely recognized as a significant stream of Buddhist teaching. Its influence continues to grow as the sophistication of its worldview and its provision of spiritual support for ordinary people in all dimensions of life becomes better known. This introduction focuses on Hōnen (1133-1212; Buddhist name: Genkū), a pioneering leader among the numerous teachers in China and Japan, who brought Pure Land teaching to the masses in an effective and enduring way. Hōnen's life represents the crisis of the age in which he lived.[1] It was a time of growing violence and turbulence which transformed his life, as it did hosts of Japanese. As a young child he had to flee, taking refuge in a temple, when his father was assassinated in 1142 as the result of a dispute over land. According to tradition, the dying father requested his son to pray for his soul and not to take vengeance.

Whatever the case, Hōnen entered the religious life in 1145 on Mount Hiei and a few years later on he settled in the Kurodani area famous for its connections to Pure Land practice. While there he studied the various schools of Buddhism and in his religious quest became most attracted to Pure Land *Nembutsu* practice of reciting the name of Amida Buddha. Dissatisfied with spiritual conditions on Mount Hiei, he established his own center at Yoshimizu in the Higashiyama area of Kyoto where he developed in earnest his teaching of the sole practice of *Nembutsu* influenced by the teaching of the Chinese master Shan-tao [Zendō in Japanese] (613-681).

Drawn by Shan-tao's comprehensive teaching on the *Nembutsu*, Hōnen launched the independent Jōdo sect, believing that it would be the most spiritually effective path for his degenerate age. As a result of his character and struggles, he also became a cultural icon and symbol of compassion in the broader society. In this brief introductory essay we will focus on Hōnen's achievement in making Pure Land teaching a major religious and social force in Japan through the efforts of his successors.

[1] Hōnen's life transpired during the final years of the Heian Period (794-1185), dominated by the court in Kyoto, and the Kamakura Period (1185-1332), when the warrior clans gained control of the society. The struggle of the Taira and Minamoto clans for hegemony in this time was marked by violence and tragedy. Hōnen's life reflects the changing situation.

The Impact of Hōnen's Teaching

Hōnen's teaching struck a chord in people's hearts because the turmoil of the age made them more aware of their own defilements, the brevity of life, and anxiety for their welfare after death. His teaching, based on his own experience, was decidedly otherworldly. He persistently taught the power of *Nembutsu*—based on Amida's Vow to overcome all obstacles to Enlightenment—for everyone, whether a highly competent monk, scholar, aristocrat, warrior, a lowly peasant, fisherman, robber, or even a prostitute. In Hōnen we see a man of great warmth and humane feeling, which he communicated to every individual he met, no matter what status the person held. Many examples are provided by Hōnen's biography. Sincere recitation of the *Nembutsu* would purify a person, high or low, of eons of *kalpas* (inconceivably long periods of time) of evils.

As an illustration of his compassion, among the samurai warrior converts, Kumagai Jirō Naozane stands out. He is famous as a symbol for the violence of the age by his beheading the Taira youth, Atsumori, during the battle between the Taira and the Genji at Ichi-no-tani. This story has been immortalized in a touching scene in the *Heike Monogatari* and in the Noh play *Atsumori*. Kumagai, desiring to spare the unknown warrior whom he encountered, was forced to fight and slay him because of the warrior's own insistence on combat and the fact that Kumagai's companions would have done it anyway. When he took the head, he was struck by remorse because of the age of the youth, his refinement, possessing a flute, and his courage. The trauma caused him to repent of his many killings. Fear of his future doom in hell motivated him to become a devoted monk following Hōnen.[2]

While the dramatic story of Kumagai and Atsumori became the stuff of literature, Kumagai's relationship with Hōnen is more complex. Because of some conflict, Yoritomo confiscated his property, leading him to become a monk with the name of Rensei. Hōnen's response in about 1204 to a now lost letter of Kumagai is the only clearly historical information available. In the letter Hōnen discusses the relation of *Nembutsu* and other practices. Essentially his instruction is that Kumagai should recite the *Nembutsu* as

[2] See Helen Craig McCullough, trans., *Heike Monogatari*, sections 10 and 16. http://www.glopac.org/Jparc/Atsumori/Heiketxt.htm. For the Noh play *Atsumori*, see http://www.sacred-texts.com/shi/npj/npj08.htm. For the story of his conversion, see Harper H. Coates and Ryugaku Ishizuka, *Honen the Buddhist Saint: His Life and Teaching*, vol. III, pp. 488-489 [pp. 103-104 in the 2006 World Wisdom (WW) edition]. No mention is made of the battle; only his evil is emphasized.

much as 60,000 times a day and if he is able, he can do other practices as well. He may also observe precepts if he desires. He also comments that if he practices *Nembutsu* sincerely and diligently, he will still be saved even if there is some infraction.[3]

Another famous convert is the harlot whom Hōnen met on his way to exile. The incident recalls the story of the woman accused of adultery in the New Testament, whom Jesus does not condemn but exhorts to go and sin no more (John 8:1-11). The woman in Hōnen's biography finally settled in a village and devoted herself to the *Nembutsu*, rejoicing that it could save even one like her.[4]

As the thrust of Hōnen's teaching became clearer in its implicit egalitarianism and transcendence of institution, criticisms of, and resistance to, his message emerged. Nevertheless, everyone had to recognize his sincerity and that in an increasingly chaotic world, his teaching gave hope of a blessed alternative to this world and an escape from the terrors of the afterlife through the embrace of Amida Buddha's compassion. In the biography by Shunjō, excerpted in this volume, many accounts are given of individuals touched by Amida's compassion through their encounter with Hōnen.

Establishment of the Jōdo Sect: The Treatise on the *Nembutsu* of the Select Primal Vow

In recent years (1998) the Jōdo sect commemorated the 800th anniversary of Hōnen's inauguration of the movement inspired by the composition of his *The Treatise on the* Nembutsu *of the Select Primal Vow* (*Senchaku hongan nembutsu shū*; abbr. *Senchakushū*). This text is important as the founding manifesto of the Jōdo (Pure Land) denomination in Japan. A translation has now been published through the cooperation of the Sōgo Bukkyō Kenkyūjō of Taisho University and the University of Hawaii Press.[5] Other important works on Hōnen have also been published such as Soho Machida's, *The Ren-*

[3] Alan Andrews, unpublished manuscript on the *Life and Thought of Hōnen*, p. 43. Professor Andrews taught at the University of Vermont and was a leading scholar of Pure Land and Hōnen studies.

[4] Coates and Ishizuka, *Honen the Buddhist Saint: His Life and Teaching*, vol. IV, pp. 611-612 [p. 123 WW edition].

[5] Kuroda Institute, *Hōnen's Senchakushū: Passages on the Selection of the Nembutsu in the Original Vow* [*Senchaku Hongan Nembutsu Shū*] (Tokyo: Sōgo Bukkyō Kenkyūjō, Taisho University/Honolulu: University of Hawaii Press, 1998).

egade Monk,[6] and most recently Jonathan Watts and Yoshiharu Tomatsu's, *Traversing the Pure Land Path: A Lifetime of Encounters with Hōnen Shōnin*,[7] giving accounts of the diverse people who experienced a transformation in their lives on meeting Hōnen.

As we have noted above, Hōnen established the popular, independent movement of Pure Land teaching, advocating belief in the power of the Vow and recitation of the *Nembutsu* as the sole means for birth in Amida Buddha's Pure Land in this degenerate age. However, regard for Hōnen's teaching was not universal. Jien, the Tendai Abbot of Mount Hiei (1155-1225), in his volume *Gukanshō*, a medieval interpretation of Japanese history, viewed him as possessed by a demon and considered his teaching as immoral. He declared:

> Another case of demon possession was that of the saint with the priestly name of Hōnen (1133-1212) who has lived at the capital in recent years—during the Ken'ei era (1206-1207). He established the Invocation-of-the-Buddha's-Name (*Nembutsu*) teaching. Using the slogan "*Nembutsu* is the only teaching," he [Hōnen] maintained that people should simply praise one Buddha (Amitābha [Amida]), not practicing other Buddhist teachings, esoteric or exoteric. This strange teaching was embraced by priests and nuns who lacked wisdom and were foolish. But the teaching was very popular and spread rapidly. . . . According to my understanding of this phenomenon, there are two types of demons: the deceptive (*jumma*) and the antagonistic (*gyakuma*). Deceptive demons were responsible for such pathetic teachings as Hōnen's.[8]

The popularity of Hōnen's teaching particularly infuriated Nichiren (1221-1289), the founder of the Nichiren sect. Though perhaps exaggerated, he complained bitterly of its spread among all levels of society and wrote texts condemning its practice:

[6] Soho Machida, *Renegade Monk: Hōnen and Japanese Pure Land Buddhism* (Berkeley: University of California Press, 1999).

[7] Jonathan Watts and Yoshiharu Tomatsu (eds.), *Traversing the Pure Land Path: A Lifetime of Encounters with Honen Shonin* (Tokyo: Jōdoshū Press, 2005).

[8] Delmer M. Brown and Ichiro Ishida (trans.), *The Future and the Past: A Translation and Study of the Gukanshō, An Interpretative History of Japan Written in 1219* (Berkeley: University of California Press, 1979), pp. 171-172.

> Thanks to Hōnen's tome, people have turned away from Shākyamuni toward Amida in the faraway West, away from Shākyamuni's Bodhisattvas, Bhaisajyaguru, away from all scriptures but the Pure Land *Triad Sūtras*, away from all temples other than Amida's. They turn away monks unless they are Pure Land sectarians. Temples are disintegrating: their moss-grown roofs resemble pine trees, and only the thinnest strands of smoke are to be seen; the cells are dilapidated, and in the wild grass the dew is deep. And yet people have reconstructed neither the temples nor their faith; thus neither holy monks nor benevolent gods have returned to the temples. Hōnen is to blame. Alas, for the past few decades, hundreds, thousands, ten thousands have been waylaid by the demonic phantasmagoria and have lost sight of the sacred laws. If they have turned away from the central *Lotus Sūtra* toward the marginal *Nembutsu*, is it any surprise that the gods rage while demons take courage? A thousand prayers will not avert disaster; instead may we seal this one evil.[9]

He further claimed that following the Pure Land teaching would lead a person to hell, authoring the *Treatise on* Nembutsu *and Eternal Hell* (*Nembutsu muken jigoku shō*) to demonstrate it.[10] Myōe Shōnin (1173-1232) criticized Hōnen's teaching in his text *Suppressing False Dharma* (*Zaijarin*) as an erroneous interpretation and a betrayal of Buddhism.[11] The Zen master Dōgen (1200-1253), founder of the Sōtō Zen sect in Japan, critiqued what must have been Pure Land teaching when he declared: "Most people in this world say: 'I have the desire to study Buddhism; yet the world is degenerate and man, inferior. The training Buddhism requires is too strenuous for me. I

[9] Quoted in Soho Machida, "The Exclusive *Nembutsu* (*senju-nembutsu*) as Liberation Theology," from *Showa teihon Nichiren Shōnin ibun*, ed. Risshō Daigaku Nichiren Kyōgaku Kenkyū-sho (Yamanashi: Kuon-ji, 1965), vol. 1, pp. 216-217. See also http://www.jsri.jp/English/Jodoshu/conferences/AAS/machida.html.

[10] Nichiren's condemnation of the Pure Land teaching was part of his general criticism of Japanese Buddhism. He believed that the *Lotus Sūtra* was the final and supreme teaching of Buddhism, following the Tendai interpretation of Buddha's life taught on Mount Hiei. In the case of Pure Land teaching, he believed it slandered Shākyamuni because the Pure Land Sūtras derived from an earlier stage of Buddha's teaching and were superseded. In addition, Amida Buddha became the focus of devotion in place of the Eternal Shākyamuni of the *Lotus Sūtra*. To slander a Buddha causes one to fall into eternal hell.

[11] Hōnen appeared to betray Buddhism because he allegedly rejected the principle of the "aspiration for Enlightenment" (*bodaishin*, Bodhi mind). This aspiration was considered the *sine qua non* for motivating the Buddhist disciple. Hōnen appeared to reduce Buddhism to the mere vocalization of the name.

will follow the easy way and merely strengthen my links with Buddhism and put off enlightenment until another life.'" Dōgen responded to this view: "The attitude these words express is completely wrong."[12] In his text *Bendowa*, he wrote concerning *Nembutsu*:

> Constant repetition of the *Nembutsu* is also worthless—like a frog in a spring field croaking night and day. Those deluded by fame and fortune, find it especially difficult to abandon the *Nembutsu*. Bound by deep roots to a profit-seeking mind, they existed in ages past, and they exist today. They are to be pitied.[13]

It is clear from these responses that Hōnen had a distinctive influence in medieval society, arousing enmity or steadfast devotion. Shinran (1173-1262), one of his six or seven direct disciples and the founder of the Jōdo Shinshū denomination, testifies to Hōnen's crucial influence on his life. Since this author is most familiar with Shinran, we offer him as example of the devotion inspired by Hōnen's work.

Shinran's Encounter with Hōnen

Shinran had struggled for twenty years from the age of nine to gain Enlightenment on Mount Hiei. Unable to attain his goal and despairing of his future destiny he turned to Hōnen, whose teaching gave him an assurance that, evil as he might be, he could be saved by the *Nembutsu* grounded in Amida Buddha's Vow. Hōnen permitted him to copy his *Senchakushū* and also to draw a portrait as a sign that Shinran was a disciple.[14]

> I, Gutoku Shinran, disciple of Shākyamuni, discarded sundry practices and took refuge in the Primal Vow in 1201. In 1205 Master Genkū, out of his benevolence, granted me permission to copy his *Passages on the* Nembutsu *Selected in the Primal Vow*. In the same year, on the fourteenth day of the fourth month, the master inscribed [the copy] in his

[12] Reiho Masunaga, trans., *A Primer of Sōtō Zen: A Translation of Dōgen's Shōbōgenzō Zuimonki* (Honolulu: East West Center Press, 1971), p. 72.

[13] *Bendōwa* translation: http://www.zenki.com/bendo01.htm. See webpage http://zenki.com for more information on Sōtō Zen.

[14] *The Collected Works of Shinran* (Kyoto: Jōdo Shinshū Hongwanji-ha, 1997), I, p. 290, #118.

own hand with an inside title, *Passages on the* Nembutsu *Selected in the Primal Vow*, with the words, "*Namu Amida Butsu*: as the act that leads to birth in the Pure Land, the *Nembutsu* is taken to be fundamental," and with [the name he had bestowed on me,] "Shakkū, disciple of Shākyamuni." That day, my request to borrow his portrait was granted, and I made a copy. During that same year, on the twenty-ninth day of the seventh intercalary month, the master inscribed my copy of the portrait with "*Namu Amida Butsu*" and with a passage expressing the true teaching.

Shinran also extols his teacher in his *Hymns on the Pure Land Masters*:

> As our teacher Genkū appeared in the world
> And spread the One Vehicle of the universal Vow,
> Throughout the entire country of Japan
> Favorable conditions for the Pure Land teaching emerged.
>
> Our teacher Genkū appeared
> Through the power of the Light of Wisdom,
> And revealing the true Pure Land way,
> He taught the selected Primal Vow.
>
> Though Shan-tao and Genshin urged all to enter the true Pure Land way,
> If our teacher Genkū had not spread it among us
> On these isolated islands in this defiled age,
> How could we ever have awakened to it?[15]

However, because of differences in the interpretation of Hōnen's teaching with other successors of Hōnen, Shinran has traditionally not been regarded by the official Jōdo sect as a successor of Hōnen.[16] Modern research, however, has established their historical relationship.[17]

[15] *The Collected Works of Shinran*, "Hymns of the Pure Land Masters," #98-100.

[16] Coates and Ishizuka, *Honen the Buddhist Saint: His Life and Teaching*, vol. I, pp. 48-49.

[17] Shinran's references to Hōnen are his own witness to their relationship. It was not until 1921 that there was external evidence provided by Shinran's wife, Eshin-ni's letters, which were discovered in the Nishi Hongwanji storehouse in Kyoto. See Yoshiko Ohtani, *The Life of Eshinni: Wife of Shinran Shōnin* (1980), pp. 91-94, Letter 3.

Eventually, the teacher and disciple were separated by exile, never to meet again. Nevertheless, Shinran continued to be inspired by Hōnen's spirit, maintaining constantly that Hōnen was the source of his teaching. It became the motivation for his own effort to propagate the teaching of Amida Buddha's unconditional compassion and wisdom.

The Socio-Religious Significance of Hōnen's Nembutsu *Teaching*

In its simplest expression of faith in *Nembutsu* as the means for rebirth in the Western Paradise, the Pure Land teaching has largely been viewed, and often devalued, as an otherworldly faith focused on the afterlife, as we see in Dōgen's statement above. For an ancient people, however, living in an unpredictable world of wars, famines, natural disasters, and the exactions of despotic rulers, the prospects of a future life of bliss was very attractive. For those bound to land and family and unable to enjoy the tranquility of monasteries in order to pursue Enlightenment, the easy practice of *Nembutsu* at home or in the field offered an inviting alternative that helped make a difficult life bearable.

Hōnen's teaching focused on the most elemental aspect of religion. What saves people is not the elaborate doctrines, organizations, rituals, and institutions of traditional religion, but the basic attitude of the heart. He summarized his view in a famous document written toward the end of his life, *Testimony on One Sheet of Paper* (*Ichimai Kishōmon*):

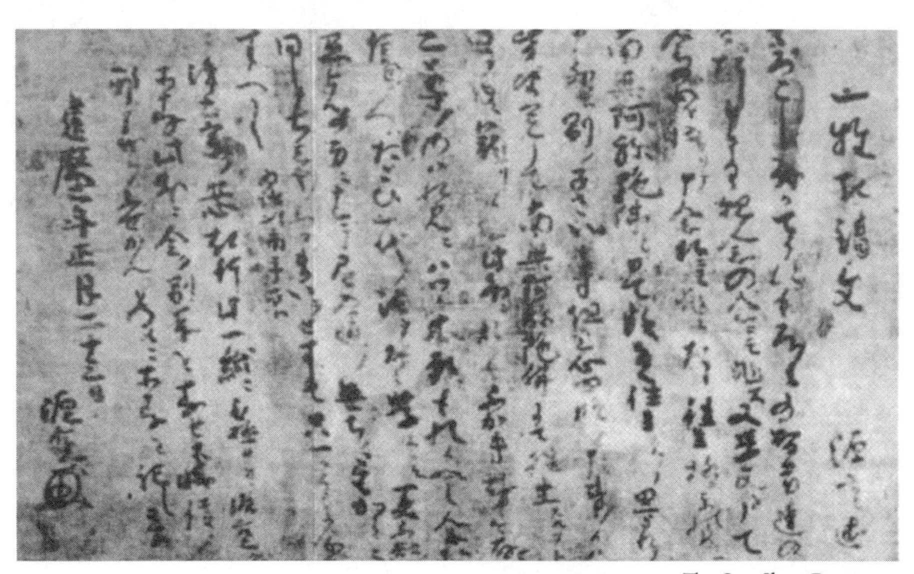

The One Sheet Document

> The method of final salvation that I have propounded is neither a sort of meditation, such as has been practiced by many scholars in China and Japan, nor is it a repetition of the Buddha's name by those who have studied and understood the deep meaning of it. It is nothing but the mere repetition of the "*Namu Amida Butsu*," without a doubt of his mercy whereby one may be born into the Pure Land of Bliss. The mere repetition with firm faith includes all the practical details, such as the threefold preparation of mind and the four practical rules. If I as an individual have any doctrine more profound than this, I should miss the mercy of the two Honorable ones, Amida and Shaka [Shākyamuni], and be left out of the Vow of the Amida Buddha. Those who believe this, though they clearly understand all the teachings Shaka taught throughout his whole life, should behave themselves like simple-minded folk, who know not a single letter, or like ignorant nuns or monks whose faith is implicitly simple. Thus without pedantic airs, they should fervently practice the repetition of the name of Amida and that alone.[18]

The path of *Nembutsu* faith advocated by Hōnen also rendered unnecessary the wealthy, ornate temples and rituals sponsored by the nobility. The establishment of the magnificent temples such as the Byōdōin in Kyoto were chiefly designed to secure a blessed hereafter for the nobility.[19] Now, however, ordinary people could carry Amida Buddha with them symbolically in the recitation of his name and receive all the benefits of the Pure Land through their simple faith. Many stories told in popular tales recounted the efficacy of the *Nembutsu* to bring about rebirth for even ordinary people.[20] In a way we might compare his view of direct salvation through *Nembutsu* with Luther's teaching of the priesthood of all believers which displaced the monopoly of the means of salvation by the established Church institution.

[18] Coates and Ishizuka, *Honen the Buddhist Saint: His Life and Teaching*, vol. V, pp. 728-729 [p. 135 WW edition].

[19] A villa of Fujiwara Michinaga, a powerful regent during the Heian period, it was turned into a temple by his son Yorimichi in 1052.

[20] There grew up from the seventh century in China and then from the tenth century in Japan a genre of literature known as Biographies of Birth in the Pure Land (*Ōjōden*) of Amitābha, or other Buddhas and Bodhisattvas. The legendary stories included lay people as well as monks and contributed to the legitimization of popular Pure Land practice. See Mark Blum, abstract: http://www.l.u-tokyo.ac.jp/iahr2005/iahrabst.htm and Jodo-shu Research Inst. Five Chinese Masters of Jōdo-shū: http://www.jsri.jp/English/Pureland/LINEAGE/china.html.

We must note here that Hōnen did not invent the *Nembutsu*, nor was he the first to advocate disseminating it among the masses. His achievement was to raise the *Nembutsu* to the position of the central practice offered by Amida Buddha to the exclusion of all other practices dedicated to other Buddhas or Bodhisattvas. He argued, following the teaching of Shan-tao, that it was *the* means selected by Amida because it was based on his Vow.[21]

Prior to Hōnen's elevation of Amida's Pure Land as the central teaching of Buddhism, Pure Land faith was a dimension of Japanese Buddhism in all schools, available as a source of hope for ordinary people. However, it was considered a secondary or compassionate means offered by the Buddha for the less spiritually competent. It created no conflict with other teachings but was promoted as part of the complex of ancestral religion to take care of the dead.

During the centuries before Hōnen there had been sporadic efforts to promote the *Nembutsu* more widely among the people without opposition or criticism. Kūya Shōnin (903-972), the "Saint of the marketplace" and Ryōnin (1073-1132), a Tendai monk and the founder of the Yūzū *Nembutsu* school, are noted for their efforts to help ordinary people. Ryōnin's teaching is interesting for its inclusive character and its employment of the central Buddhist principle of interdependence in propagating the *Nembutsu*. Each individual's *Nembutsu* helps the other's and each other's *Nembutsu* helps all other individuals. It is based on the Kegon and Tendai concept of mutual interpenetration of all aspects of reality applied concretely to the method of salvation.

There were also aristocratic fraternities of lay people devoted to the Pure Land teaching that had been organized by the Abbot Genshin on Mount Hiei. They focused on the *Amida Sūtra* and the last thought at death, and were involved with funerals and memorials for the dead.[22] Wandering holy men (*hijiri*) also carried *Nembutsu* faith throughout Japan, preparing the

[21] It was Shan-tao who changed the reading of the Eighteenth Vow of Amida from its original reading, which included the practice of meditation, to the practice of recitation of the name and thus furthered the popular development of *Nembutsu* teaching. The Chinese text reads: "If, when I become Buddha, all the beings of the universe are not born into my Pure Land when they think on me for even as few as ten thoughts, with sincerity, trusting faith, and desire to be born (there), I will not accept the highest enlightenment." However, Shan-tao read the text: ". . . if when I become Buddha, all beings are not reborn, as they recite my name even down to ten voicings, may I not gain true enlightenment" (Quoted in Alfred Bloom, *Shinran's Gospel of Pure Grace* [Tucson, AZ: The University of Arizona Press, 1968], p. 15).

[22] Saburo Ienaga, ed., *Bukkyōshi* (Kyoto: Hōzōkan, 1972), I, pp. 239-240.

way for the later success of Hōnen and his disciples. These holy men were recluses who retired to mountains and valleys, sincerely treading the Buddhist path while rejecting fame and profit. Among the famous places for them to gather was Yogawa and Kurodani on Mount Hiei.[23]

Viewed from a broader perspective, Hōnen's teaching was a natural development of the evolution of Pure Land teaching from ancient times in East Asia. Initially, Amida Buddha was simply one among many Buddhas who provided a focus for meditation and spiritual aspiration. There was a comprehensiveness and universality inherent in the Amida teaching that contributed to its gradual rise to dominance as a popular movement. Over the centuries numerous masters such as T'an-luan (476-542) and Tao-ch'o (562-645) interpreted the teaching as a way for ordinary people, as well as monks. In the process of popularization the Pure Land teaching became associated with the theory of the Last Age in the Demise of the Dharma (*mappō*). According to this teaching, there are three stages from the time of the true Dharma given by Shākyamuni: (1) the semblance or counterfeit Dharma, (2) a time when there was teaching and practice but no realization, and (3) the Last Age. In the Last Age the Dharma is neither taught, practiced, nor realized; it is a time of decay, division, and disruption in Buddhism, thought to begin, in one theory, in 552 and in another, widely accepted in Japan, in 1052. The last period would endure ten thousand years. However, during this final age the teaching of Amida Buddha appears as a refuge for spiritually impotent, decadent, and suffering people.

With Shan-tao, however, Amida became the central object of worship, while other Buddhist divinities remained auxiliary. Amida was the chief Buddha. With the appearance of Hōnen, Amida became the superior Buddha and the sole source of salvation for this age.

Through Hōnen's famous manifesto, *The Treatise on the* Nembutsu *of the Select Primal Vow* (*Senchakushū*) composed in 1198 at the request of his major supporter, the Prime Minister Tsukinowa Kujō Kanezane, he established the independent Pure Land movement with persuasive textual and doctrinal support for the *Nembutsu* as the sole means for salvation in the Last Age. According to Hōnen, this method was specifically designated by Amida Buddha in his Eighteenth Vow for all people, irrespective of their social or religious status, in the degenerate, corrupt Last Age. It was not simply

[23] Kasahara Kazuo and Kawasaki Yasushi, *Shūkyōshi* (Tokyo: Yamakawa Shuppansha, 1966), p. 123.

an auxiliary or subordinate practice among the many methods of Buddhist discipline as taught in other traditions, but rather, *the* means selected by Amida Buddha for *all* people ultimately to achieve Enlightenment.

It was a ringing challenge to the traditional Buddhist establishment, which, when it became known, immediately responded with angry denunciations and demands to prohibit Hōnen's teaching. However, it also inspired devotion among his followers who found spiritual liberation through it.

If we look into the *Senchakushū* we can discover the clues to Hōnen's religious and social significance:

1. Hōnen placed the Pure Land teaching of *Nembutsu* among the Mahāyāna sects by employing the method of doctrinal distinctions. By outlining the features of his system of teaching in contrast to other approaches, a teacher establishes a new sect, demonstrating the truth or superiority of his doctrine and practice. The formation of such a classification of teachings was essential for establishing an independent sect within the diversity of Mahāyāna Buddhism. It was also necessary to clarify one's lineage in the tradition.

Hōnen also selected out of the wealth of Pure Land tradition three major Sūtras which were central to Pure Land teaching as the basis of his sect: *The Larger Pure Land Sūtra* (also called *The Larger Sūtra*); *The Sūtra on the Contemplation of the Buddha of Eternal Life* (also called *The Contemplation Sūtra*); and *The Amida Sūtra* (also called *The Smaller Pure Land Sūtra*). *The Larger Sūtra* recounted the story of the Bodhisattva Dharmākara and the Vows which led to his attainment of Buddhahood as Amida and the foundation of the Pure Land. *The Contemplation Sūtra* presented the practice of recitation of the name as the way for birth in the Pure Land for the lowest grade of foolish beings, as well as modes of meditation. *The Amida Sūtra* described the Pure Land and also affirmed recitation.

Hōnen's achievement in the *Senchakushū* was also to provide a doctrinal foundation for the teaching of the sole practice of *Nembutsu*, going a step beyond Shan-tao in China, who still recognized the utility of the practice of meditation or visualization in monastic discipline.

The set of critical distinctions for establishing the Pure Land sect were taken from the Pure Land tradition. Over the centuries a variety of contrasting terms had grown up to distinguish the Pure Land teaching from others. These included the path of easy practice-difficult practice (derived from Nāgārjuna [150-250]), Self-Power and Other-Power (T'an-luan), the Pure

Land Gate (teaching) and the Saintly Path teaching (Tao-ch'o), and Shan-tao's distinction of right practice (chanting Sūtras, meditation, worship, recitation of the name, and offerings) based on sole devotion to Amida versus the mixed or miscellaneous practices directed to other objects of worship. Shan-tao further distinguished among the right practices, designating the practice of recitation as the rightly determined practice in contrast to assisting or auxiliary practices to amplify the effectiveness of the recitation. Shan-tao had interpreted the recitation of the name as the practice designated by the Eighteenth Vow and thereby a central practice of Pure Land tradition. The sole recitation of the name of Amida Buddha became the focus for Hōnen's teaching and his followers.

In the *Senchakushū*, Hōnen brought all these distinctions together to proclaim that Pure Land teaching was the sole vehicle for salvation in the Last Age (*mappō*) for everyone, whether common people or elite monks. The *Nembutsu* was universal and within the capacity of any person, while all other practices required some special ability, religious, intellectual, moral, or even financial.

Standing on the shoulders of the cumulative and pervasive tradition of Pure Land teaching, Hōnen gave it definition as a distinctive sect among the traditionally accepted Buddhist institutions of Japan. His disciples carried on their teacher's perspective, each developing his own style of teaching and practice.

2. A second significant aspect related to the issue of critical distinctions of doctrine is the concept of *senchaku*, which describes the process of selection and rejection. Hōnen observed closely the foundational story of Bodhisattva Dharmākara's survey of all Buddha Lands and universes in *The Larger Pure Land Sūtra*. The Bodhisattva's Forty-Eight Primal (Fundamental) Vows, a selection of the best features of all worlds, became the basis for his construction of an ideal world where all beings could achieve Enlightenment and spiritual liberation. This world became the Western Pure Land, the goal of Pure Land devotion where Dharmākara Bodhisattva *qua* Amida Buddha resides. Hōnen connected the formation of the critical distinctions in doctrine to the story of Bodhisattva Dharmākara, giving the Pure Land teaching a stronger scriptural basis.

He also implied that a decisive element in religious consciousness is choice. Religious faith always involves choosing. It is the choice of the most universal, and deepest understanding of, or approach to, reality. It also expresses the exclusivism or centrality of commitment that lays the basis for a strong religious personality. This can be seen in Hōnen himself, as well as his disciples, some of whom were executed, and in his successors, as well as Shinran, the later Ippen (1239-1289), founder of the Pure Land Ji sect and Rennyo (1415-1499), Eighth Abbot of the Jōdo Shinshū Hongwanji sect. Pure Land teaching is often associated with weak personality because of the stress on Other-Power, understood as an exterior power. However, confidence in Other-Power as the essence of life can be the basis for firm dedication and devotion, when one believes that reality, Amida Buddha, has embraced one's life and Amida is understood as one's true self.

3. Thirdly, the social perspective of Hōnen's thought is eloquently expressed in the passage that describes the real intent of Amida Buddha's Vows. Hōnen has stated it clearly in his own words in the *Senchakushū* to which we can add little:

> In the next place, if we look at it from the standpoint of difficulty and ease, the *Nembutsu* is easily practiced, while it is very hard to practice all the other disciplines. For the above reasons thus briefly stated, we may say that the *Nembutsu*, being so easily practiced, is of universal application. . . . If the Original Vow required the making of images and the building of pagodas, then the poor and destitute could have no hope of attaining it. But the fact is that the wealthy and noble are few in number, whereas the number of the poor and ignoble is extremely large. If the Original Vow required wisdom and great talent, there would be no hope of that birth for the foolish and ignorant at all; but the wise are few in number, while the foolish are very many. . . . We conclude therefore, that Amida Nyorai, when He was a priest by the name of Hōzō [Dharmākara] ages ago, in His compassion for all sentient beings alike, and in His effort for the salvation of all, did not vow to require the making of images or the building of pagodas conditions for birth into the Pure Land, but only the one act of calling upon His sacred name.[24]

This eloquent passage offers a social critique of the elites of his time. Hōnen is making it abundantly clear that there is no discrimination in Amida's Vow based on the accidents of birth, abilities, or social standing. It is probably this aspect of Hōnen's teaching that most threatened the established Buddhist Orders and led to the prohibition of his movement in accord

[24] Coates and Ishizuka, *Honen the Buddhist Saint: His Life and Teaching*, vol. V, p. 344 [p. 66 WW edition]. See also Kuroda Institute, *Hōnen's Senchakushū*, pp. 77-78.

with the Kōfukuji and Mount Hiei petitions to the Court. These demands, together with alleged crimes of a few disciples, brought about Hōnen's exile along with his chief disciples. The Kōfukuji petition[25] accused Hōnen of starting a new sect without government permission, subverting society by rejecting the *kami* (Japanese Shinto gods), and abandoning all other good deeds and practices other than the *Nembutsu*. According to the entreaty, Hōnen's movement resulted in the decline of other sects, which were based on the union of Buddhism and the State.

4. Another implication of the text, which is not explicitly stated, is the emancipation of Pure Land followers from the garden of magic through the concentration of devotion to Amida. Sole devotion to Amida Buddha, with its implied superiority over all other Buddhas and gods, displaced the importance of the general popular religion in securing material or worldly benefits, which was and is a major part of Japanese religion. Although Hōnen and his disciples often exhorted their followers to respect the gods and Buddhas, Hōnen gave no actual role to the *kami* in support of his teaching.

The attitude often taken by Hōnen's followers is illustrated by an incident recorded in the *Shasekishū*, where Shinto priests threatened to curse a farmer who transgressed on their land. He replied: "I have nothing to fear. Go ahead and curse me. We Pure Land Buddhists think nothing of divinity. The *kami* (gods) cannot punish those of us who do not bask in their light."[26]

The outcome was the emancipation of the peasants from spiritual oppression, based on the fear of *batchi* or divine retribution in forms of punishment if they did not obey the demands of their overlords, the temples, shrines, and *daimyo* (local warlords), who represented the divine powers on the land. Their release from superstition later led to the single-minded peasant revolts (*ikkō ikki*) in the time of Rennyo (1415-1499).

Conclusion

In our modern age we often call striking and influential teachings "revolutionary." Although this term may be too strong when we reflect on the na-

[25] James C. Dobbins, *Jōdo Shinshū: Shin Buddhism in Medieval Japan* (Bloomington, IN: Indiana University Press, 1989), pp. 14-15. Jōdoshū Research Institute: http://www.jsri.jp/English/Honen/LIFE/Last%20Days/kofukuji.html.

[26] Quoted in Machida, *Renegade Monk*, p. 6.

ture of modern revolutions, nevertheless, we may apply the term to Hōnen's work and the *Senchakushū* because even his enemies saw its potential in transforming the religious situation in Japan.[27] Consequently, they reacted vehemently and violently. At a later time, the monks of Mount Hiei violated Hōnen's grave and burned copies of his writings. While Hōnen was a pioneer, the implications of his thought, in later times, broadened the boundaries of hope for all people. In our present day, it is important to rekindle the spirit that motivated him and his critical insight and attitude to society, if the ordinary person is to find meaning and hope in the desolate wasteland of modern, secular society.

Modern people need not only Hōnen's message of hope in the afterlife but a direction for their everyday lives, lived in awareness of Amida Buddha's compassionate embrace, and motivated by the recitation of the *Nembutsu* as the focus of our minds and hearts.

ALFRED BLOOM
Emeritus Professor
University of Hawaii

[27] Machida, *Renegade Monk*, pp. 4-9, compares Hōnen's teaching to Christian liberation theology with its implicit threat to the power structure.

Shinran Shōnin

The Buddha Amida with forty-eight rays of light representing his merciful Forty-eight Vows

EXCERPTS FROM INTRODUCTIONS BY THE TRANSLATORS*

No one interested in Japan's modern development can afford to ignore the religious forces which have been at work throughout her history in molding her inner spirit. We offer, therefore, no apology for presenting the story of the epoch-making career and distinctive doctrinal system of Hōnen, the Buddhist saint of the twelfth century, and father of those numerous so-called "Pure Land" (Jōdo) sects, which now number among their adherents some sixteen million souls, and whose influence is so inextricably interwoven into the warp and woof of the nation's life.

As one of the great makers of medieval Japan, whose memory is still precious to a grateful people, Hōnen's name must forever stand on the scroll of fame. But the story of this great soul deserves a better fate than that of being shut up within the walls of Japanese insularity, in tomes of Chinese ideographs unintelligible to the outside world. He is worthy, moreover, of more than those brief references he has usually received, in general works on Japanese history, written for foreign readers. It is hardly to be expected, either, that historical sketches of Japanese Buddhism as a whole should devote to this one character all the space really necessary for a due appreciation of his personality and work.

While he has left an indelible mark upon the social and political life of his country, which, indeed with Hōnen left out, would remain in important respects, an unsolved riddle, it was in the sphere of religion that his great achievement was wrought. He was above all else a man of the spirit, and lived, moved, and had his being in the incessant invocation of Amida Buddha's sacred name, and the inculcation of the devout life upon all and sundry whom he could touch. As a study in religious biography and propagandism, his career must have a perennial value to all who do not exclude from their thinking the supreme human concerns.

* Editor's Note: The translators Coates and Ishizuka wrote multiple introductory pieces, totaling over one hunderd and fifty pages. What follows are reordered and adapted excerpts.

In these days of increasingly intimate international intercourse, which compels us, whether we will or no, to "look not every man upon his own things, but every man also on the things of others," our horizon of thought cannot but be enlarged, by putting ourselves back into the environment of a medieval Oriental, and living over again with him the life he lived more than seven hundred years ago. We shall then see whether, after all, there is not a oneness in human aspiration, which no racial or sectarian barriers can divide, and find fresh historical evidence that there is one "true Light which lighteneth every man coming into the world." We cannot but realize that men of all climes are kith and kin, and destined, sometime and somewhere, to discover their essential soul unity, in the noblest experiences of a living religion. Who can fail to recognize, as he reads Hōnen's story, that apart from philosophy, he had found life, which he must help others find too. As a study in the science of comparative religion, so popular in our day, our hero furnishes material with which every impartial student must reckon, if he would make his survey of influential world religions truly adequate.

Hōnen was a man of strong character and gentle disposition. He was stern with himself, striving after a strict observance of the Buddhist precepts. While he was in fact, as in name, "nature's own priest" (the original meaning of "Hōnen"), and his life is entirely identified with the priesthood, he had a wealth of warm human affection, and his happy blending of purity and compassion was not so much the product of rigorous discipline, as the outgoing of an inborn religious impulse. He was a thorough-going plebeian to the end, refusing official titles and degrees, although he was honored by men of rank, and often invited to Court by His Majesty the Emperor. When he went out, instead of taking a carriage, he always went on foot, wearing straw sandals. He chose the "simple life," spent in sequestered spots away from the bustling crowd, and the conventionalities even of priestly intercourse.

As to the historical background of the stage on which Hōnen played his part with such consummate skill, it must be said that the Japan of his day was exhausted and demoralized. The Court itself was so corrupt, that the occupants of the throne were but puppets in the hands of those powerful families, who with counterfeit patriotism planned and fought for their own clannish interests. The degeneracy of the religion of the period is illustrated, in the pompous ceremony with which the high priests won popular adulation, by confining their public prayers chiefly to petitions for material good, whether national or individual, and by the airy speculations of the more learned priests on the abstruse problems of metaphysics, instead of grappling with the practical problems of the spiritual life. The sanctions of morality and religion found faint echo in a disintegrating society and in souls rent with a great unrest.

Hōnen brought a veritable evangel to the heart-weary men of his generation, in the proclamation of salvation by faith in the Buddha Amida—the Buddha of Boundless Light and Life—whose compassionate power alone can, he said, effect the great deliverance, for which in their despair helpless mortals yearn. His religious tolerance showed itself in his treatment of the teaching of the meditative and non-meditative sects, which had down to his time held the field, as adapted only to men of superior capacity, who might possibly have lived in bygone ages, but who were all but an unknown quantity in these latter degenerate times. He saw no hope for common humanity anywhere but in that "Other-Power" impersonated in Amida Buddha.

His preaching was always attended by a religious awakening, and his propaganda found response among all classes in the community. As is so often the case with men of his fervid type, who refuse to be bound by mere respectable religious forms that have lost their original spirit, he encountered the official opposition of the clerical leaders of his day in Nara and on Mount Hiei. They said, "Hōnen runs down all the established Laws of the Buddhas, by promulgating the doctrine of the *Nembutsu*, with the result that all the sects are declining, and the practices they inculcate are coming to naught." He was finally condemned by the Government, and banished to the province of Sanuki. Even after his death, his bones were in danger of being exhumed and thrown into the Kamo river.

Successive Emperors have shown their esteem for his high character by bestowing upon him posthumous titles. The Emperor Go-Nara in 1537 gave him the title *Kōshō Daiji* (The Great Illuminator), and he was called *Enkō Daishi* (Perfect Light) by the Emperor Higashiyama in 1679; *Tōzen Daishi* (Great Disseminator of the East) was conferred upon him by the Emperor Nakamikado in 1710; *Ejō Daishi* (Highest Wisdom) by the Emperor Momozono in 1767; *Kōgaku Daishi* (Comprehensive Enlightenment) by the Emperor Kōkaku in 1811; *Jikyō Daishi* (Benign Instructor) by the Emperor Kōmei in 1860; and *Meishō* (Bright Illuminator) by the Emperor Meiji in 1911. Such recognition in such high quarters of Hōnen's place in the making of the national history must mark him out for special treatment in any complete survey of Japanese religion.

Note on the Original Manuscript and Illustrations

Within a century after Hōnen's death, his religion had become so widespread and established in the public confidence, that the retired Emperor Go-Fushimi (1288-1336) ordered a priest called Shunjō to prepare an accurate account of his life. When, at the Imperial command, Shunjō began the compilation of his work, he collected all the literary materials he could find from among Hōnen's disciples, and interviewed the aged who had known of the master. After rejecting everything that seemed unreliable, he wrote an authentic record of Hōnen's life and work in forty-eight volumes, dividing them into 237 sections, to each of which he appended a pictorial illustration, and presented the manuscript as it was to His Majesty, who, overjoyed at the completion of the work, ordered the literary men of the court to verify the accuracy of the text and polish the style. To improve the quality of the illustrations, he had them put into the hands of the Court artists, who made them all over again. When the text was complete, His Majesty began the transcription of it with his own hand, and the Bonze Emperor Go-Fushimi as well as Go-Nijō the Emperor on the throne were only too glad to join in the work. The rolls of this manuscript are still preserved in the archives of the Chion-in Temple in Kyōto.

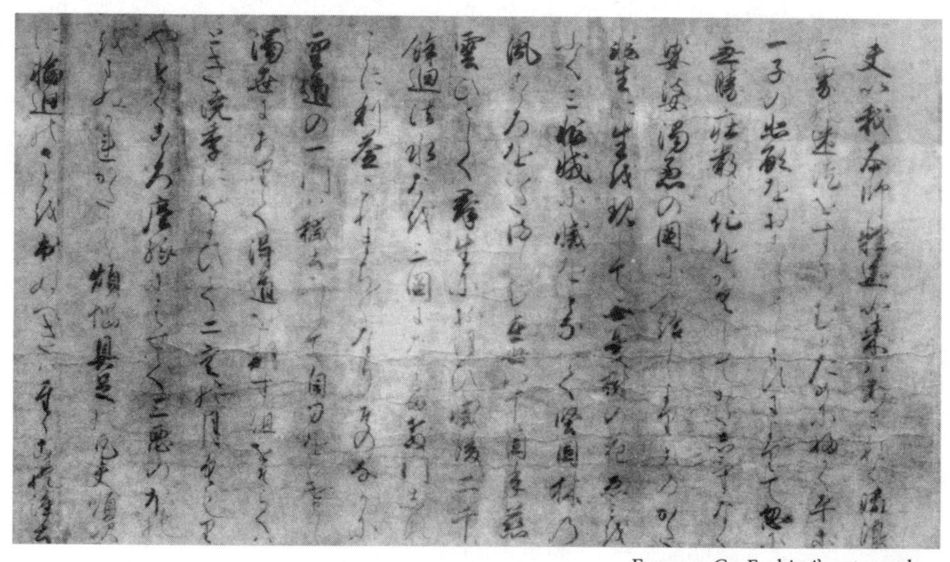

Emperor Go-Fushimi's autograph

Through the kind offices of one of the chief officials of the Chion-in temple, Dr. Coates was able to visit the temple, for three consecutive days, and examine this historic manuscript. He was more deeply impressed than ever with the great value that would be added to our book, by the insertion of a goodly number of copies of the manuscript's paintings, which are in an astonishingly fine state of preservation, even after the lapse of six centuries, and which are so beautifully illustrative of the life of our hero, and typical specimens of medieval Japanese art. The black and white collotype pictures we now present are reproductions of photographs which were taken of the original scrolls last summer (1924) by Mr. Tōdō, librarian of the Imperial University of Kyōto. For reasons of cost, we were obliged to be satisfied with but one color picture; it has been block-printed for this edition, and reproduces a hand-painted copy, performed by Mr. Shūkwa Tsuchiya, an artist famous for his painting of the *Sanjūrokkasen* (thirty-six most renowned Japanese poets who lived before the eleventh century), of the painting known as the "Halo Bridge."*

Note on the Translation

For some seventeen years, in the intervals snatched from exacting professional duties, we have together spent many quiet, profitable, and happy hours, turning the archaic literary style of the fourteenth century Japanese of Hōnen's great biography, first into modern speech and then into English, each of us good-naturedly seeking to make up for those deficiencies in the other which we have mutually recognized. Instead of projecting our own views into the record, it has seemed to us to make for greater clearness and impartiality, to keep as near as possible to the actual wording of the original. It has been a labor of love which has bound our souls together as "with hooks of steel." If we had realized at the beginning the magnitude of the task we were undertaking, we might well have shrunk from it, but we have just gone on, a step at a time, from chapter to chapter, facing each problem as it arose, until the complete translation, with historical and critical notes, stands before us.

Rev. Harper Havelock Coates &
Rev. Ryugaku Ishizuka

* Editor's Note: The majority of the illustrations from the 1925 Coates-Ishizuka edition are reproduced in the current edition. The color picture, the "Halo Bridge," is reproduced on the cover of the current edition. Certain other illustrations are new to the current edition.

The Pure Land of Amida

EXCERPTS FROM 14TH CENTURY FOREWORD

Many learned men have devoted their best talents to an exposition of the doctrines of the Pure Land, among whom was the venerable Zendō, of the T'ang dynasty (in China). But in our country, the venerable Hōnen Shōnin was, up to his day, the only one who taught that the most important thing of all is the practice of the repetition of the sacred name of the Buddha Amida. Though these two saints were of different nationalities, the one of Japan and the other of China, their method of instruction was the same, and through their influence multitudes of men and women of high degree and low alike easily attained to the life of faith, and to birth into the Pure Land, accompanied by abundant omens of purple clouds and sweet perfumes. It was then through them that the cult of the *Nembutsu* attained its highest prosperity.

Since the departure of Hōnen, many years have passed, and unless his words of instruction and warning are put on record for future generations, who, by beholding the wise man and longing to be like him, will know what is essential to salvation? For this reason, I have not only made careful enquiries regarding the things I have heard about Hōnen, but I have critically examined all the old records obtainable, I have selected among them what I believe to be true, I have corrected whatever errors I found, and have written down a succinct account of his life from beginning to end. For the easy comprehension of the unlettered, and with a view to stimulating the faith of those who read, I have filled the book with pictorial illustrations, to serve as a clear mirror in which men of every age may see their true selves. Surely none among those yearning for birth into the Pure Land will fail to appreciate the motive of my writing.

Shunjō Hōin

I.

HŌNEN'S BIOGRAPHY: EARLY YEARS UP TO FOUNDING OF THE JŌDO SECT

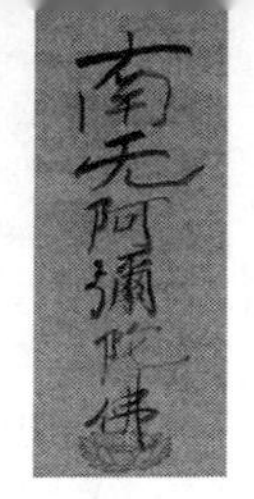

1. HŌNEN'S CHILDHOOD

Hōnen's Birth

Hōnen Shōnin[1] was born in the village of Inaoka in the southern part of the township of Kume in the province of Mimasaka. Tokikuni Uruma, his father, was the military chief (*Ōryōshi*) for the township, and his mother's maiden name was Hada. Being childless, in their grief they prayed to the Buddha and to the gods for a child, and Hada had a dream in which she thought she swallowed a razor.[2] Forthwith she found herself *enceinte*. Tokikuni, overjoyed, said to his wife, "The child in your womb will doubtless be a boy, and he is destined to become a teacher of the Emperor." Hada was a woman of gentle spirit, and during the whole period of pregnancy was quite free from pain. She strictly abstained from wine, meat, and the five prohibited vegetables,[3] ever regarding the Three Sacred Treasures[4] with deep reverence.

Mysterious Omens

At length on the seventh day of the fourth month in the second year of Chōjō (May 20, 1133), in the reign of the Emperor Sutoku, she gave painless birth to a son, precisely at the hour of the horse (12 a.m.), when a purple cloud appeared in the sky,[5] and two white banners alighted upon the profuse branches of a double trunked *muku* tree, which stood on the west side of the house within the garden enclosure, while little bells, hanging from the banners, tinkled out their joyous notes to the sky, and the luster of their patterns shone brightly in the sunbeams.

After seven days, to the amazement of all who had seen and heard, they ascended and disappeared. Thenceforth this tree was called the "two-bannered *muku* tree," and though long afterward it fell to the ground, sweet odors and other miraculous tokens did not cease. This was why the peo-

[1] Shōnin is an honorary title, meaning "the superior man whom we revere."

[2] The emblem of a spiritual teacher. The first thing done to one about to enter the priesthood was to shave his head with a razor.

[3] All kinds of the *genus allium*, such as garlic, onions, etc.

[4] The Buddha, the Law, and the Church (Sanskrit: Buddha, Dharma, and Sangha).

[5] A sign of *Ōjō*, or birth in the Pure Land of Amida Buddha.

ple regarded the place with reverence, and built here a temple which they called Tanjōji, the birth temple, with a special chapel enshrining the image of Hōnen, where they practiced the *Nembutsu.*[6] It is related that at the time of the birth of the Emperor Ōjin, four pairs of banners came down from the sky, showing it is believed, his perfect assimilation of the Noble Eightfold Path,[7] and now the phenomena attending Hōnen's birth recalled this ancient wonder, as charged with some significant meaning.

Hōnen's birth

His Childhood Name

The new-born child was named Seishi Maru. From the age when he used to play horse with a bamboo stick, his manners were more like those of a grown-up than of a child, such for instance as his habit of sitting with his face toward the west (where the Pure Land of Amida[8] lies), and his behavior during his youth seems to have resembled that of Tendai Daishi.[9]

[6] *Nembutsu*: The practice of the repetition of *Namu Amida Butsu*, "I take refuge in Amida Buddha." See Glossary under *Nembutsu.*

[7] Noble Eightfold Path: This signifies the fundamental practical moral standards taught by the historical Buddha Shākyamuni. The path has the following eight characteristics: 1) right views, 2) right thinking, 3) right words, 4) right acts, 5) right livelihood, 6) right efforts, 7) right-mindedness, 8) right meditation.

[8] The Paradise of the Buddha Amida. See Glossary under Amida Buddha and Pure Land (Jōdo).

[9] Tendai Daishi (538-597). Founder of the so-called Tendai sect in China. His lectures, especially on the *Hokke* or *Lotus Sūtra*, were written down and formed such a voluminous

His Family History If we enquire into his family history, the following facts appear. Toshi Minamoto, also called Shikibutarō, was descended from Hikaru Nishi Sanjō, one of the highest officials of the Supreme Council of State (*Udaijin*), and the seventeenth son of the Emperor Nimmyō. This Toshi murdered an official of the Imperial Archives (*Kurōdo*) called Kanetaka at the Yōmei gate of the palace. For this offence he was banished to the province of Mimasaka, where he married a daughter of Motokuni Uruma, the military chief of the township of Kume, and a son was born to them. Now as Motokuni had no male heir, he adopted this boy, and changed his name from Minamoto to Uruma, with the given name of Moriyuki. This Moriyuki had a son called Shigetoshi, and the latter had a son called Kunihiro, who in turn had a son by the name of Tokikuni.

Tokikuni's Fate This Tokikuni, being somewhat proud of his noble ancestry, was inclined to look down upon the headman of Inaoka, known as Musha Sada-akira Akashi no Gennai, and naturally did he not only fail to pay him proper respect, but became negligent of his official duties. Tokikuni even declined to meet Sada-akira when he wished to see him. The latter deeply resented such discourtesy, and one night in the spring of the seventh year of Hōen (1141) made an attempt upon Tokikuni's life. Seishi Maru, who was only nine years old at the time, escaped from his bedroom and hid himself somewhere about the house. Peeping through a small aperture, he observed Sada-akira in the garden feathering an arrow, whereupon young Seishi Maru, taking careful aim with his little arrow, struck the man right between the eyes. The resulting wound was in such a prominent place that it could not be concealed, and there was danger of suspicion being directed towards Sada-akira for the wound he had inflicted upon the boy's father. So, fearing that the relatives of Tokikuni might take revenge upon him, he ran away at lightning speed, and was never seen in the place again. Thus it came about that the boy was called "Little Arrow Boy" (*Koyago*), and people were never tired talking of his exploits.

Tokikuni's Dying Request Tokikuni's wound proved incurable, and as he drew near to the gates of death, he turned to his nine-year old boy and said, "Don't let this rankle in your breast and lead you to avenge my enemy, as was done in the well-known case

and comprehensive work that various new forms of religion later developed in Japan may all be said to have had their roots in it.

of the humiliation on Mount Kuei-chi.[10] This misfortune was the result of some sin of mine in a former state of existence. If you harbor ill-will towards your enemy, you will never be free from enemies. So don't do it, my boy, but without delay forsake the worldly life and become a priest. Then pray that I may attain Buddhahood, and seek earnestly too for your own salvation." Thus saying, he sat erect with his face to the west, folded his hands in prayer to the Buddha, and, as if falling asleep, breathed his last.

Hōnen's childhood

[10] This is an expression signifying the height of disgrace, based on an ancient Chinese story.

2. HŌNEN'S BOYHOOD

Kwangaku *Tokugō*

Now in this province there was a cloister known as Bodaiji, the abbot of which was Kwangaku, a priest who bore the honorable title of *Tokugō* (religious lecturer). As he was Hada's younger brother, he was the uncle of Seishi Maru, who, in harmony with his father's dying request, had been put under Kwangaku's care. The boy's natural aptitude for study was as quick as the swiftly flowing mountain stream. If you told him one thing he understood ten. He never forgot anything he was told.

Hōnen at his uncle's residence

The Country No Place for Such a Boy

As Kwangaku saw that the boy's talents were unusual, he thought it was too bad for such a genius to waste his time, covered up in the dust of an out-of-the-way countryside, and so, as was most fitting, he began to make preparations for sending him up to the cloud-land of Hiei, the sacred Mount of Tendai.[1] As soon as the boy heard of his uncle's intention, he had no more heart for remaining in his native place, but thought only of hastening to the capital.

[1] Another name for Mount Hiei, the sacred mountain and priestly center of the Tendai sect of Japanese Buddhism.

His Parting Words to His Mother

Kwangaku gladly went with him to his mother to talk the matter over, when the boy spoke to her in the following strain, "After many painful transmigrations, I have at length attained the glory of being born a man. In a world of illusion I have at length come face to face with the teaching of the Buddha which dispels it all. When one comes to see before one's very eyes the utter changeableness of all things, he cannot but reject the bloom-like glory of the visionary world. Above all, my father's parting words keep ringing in my ears, and I cannot forget them. And so I must at once proceed up Mount Shimei,[2] and enter upon the study of the one only Vehicle.[3] Of course, mother, as long as you live, I shall fulfill my filial duty to you morning and evening to the utmost; but as one of the Sūtras says, the best way for children to show their gratitude to their parents is by turning away from the temporal, and devoting themselves to the eternal. Let not therefore your sorrow over a morning good-bye cast its gloom over the whole day." With many such words did he comfort his mother's heart.

[2] Synonym for Mount Hiei

[3] This refers to the doctrine taught in the *Lotus Sūtra*, where the following words occur—"There is only one vehicle, not two, nor three," i.e. neither the Hīnayāna nor the Mahāyāna, but that which includes and transcends them both. The word *vehicle* means a body of doctrine on which sentient beings may ride to the other shore of perfect enlightenment. For further details see Glossary under Hīnayāna and Mahāyāna.

Hōnen and the Regent Tadamichi on the Toba road to Kyōto

The Mother's Tears of Grief She was so thoroughly convinced of the reasonableness of all he said, that she gave consent to his request, and yet she was so overwhelmed with grief that the tears ran down her sleeve upon the boy's raven locks. It was hard for her, as it always is for flesh and blood, to bear up under such sorrows, and so easy to yield to the feelings of nature which are bound to arise at a time of separation from loved ones. Her grief found expression in the following memorable lines:

> Alas for me! what shall I do when I must even part
> With this my boy,—his father's one last gift to cheer my heart!

The Letter of Introduction But in spite of all her heart protests, she sent the boy by Kwangaku to a priest called Jihōbō Genkō, who was living in the northern part of the western section of the three groups of temples on Mount Hiei. In his letter of introduction to Genkō, Kwangaku said, "I send you herewith an image of the great and revered Monju,"[4] by which he meant to indicate the boy's extraordinary ability.

[4] Sanskrit: Manjusrī, a Bodhisattva believed to be the apotheosis of transcendental wisdom.

The Boy Meets the Regent Tadamichi

Thus in his fifteenth year, like one who leaves behind him the dense mists of the work-a-day world and ascends into the beautiful cloud-land, the boy bids farewell to his country home, and comes up to the capital, on the thirteenth day of the second month of the third year of Kyūan (1147), in the reign of the Emperor Konoe. As he was passing along the Toba road to Kyōto, he met the Regent, Tadamichi Fujiwara of the Hosshōji Temple. Dismounting from his horse, he made obeisance, when the Regent ordered his carriage to be stopped, and asked who that person was. A priest accompanying the boy told who he was, whereupon the Regent courteously saluted him and passed on. At this his attendants were quite surprised, but later he said to them, "The boy we met by the way had a peculiar light in his eyes, and I am sure he is of no common mold. That is why I saluted him." And when we come to think of it, may not the fact that his son Kanezane of Tsukinowa became an earnest believer in Hōnen, have been due to the deep impression left on his mind by hearing this story from his father. It is indeed quite possible.

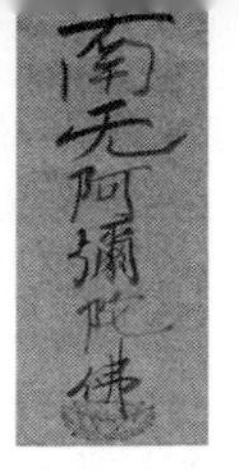

3. HIS STUDIES ON MOUNT HIEI

His Ascent of the Mountain

On the boy's arrival at the capital, he sent a messenger with the letter from his uncle to Jihōbō Genkō, who on reading it asked where the image of Monju was. When the messenger told him that it was only a boy who had come up to the capital, Genkō at once knew that the boy must be very clever, and sent for him. So he came up Mount Hiei on the fifteenth day of the second month in the same year.

Hōnen climbing Mount Hiei

He Studies the *Shikyōgi* under Genkō

Leaving the charming capital, he climbed the steep and arduous path up the mountainside, and entered the study of Jihōbō, who, to test the boy's ability, first of all began to teach him the *Shikyōgi* (On the Four Doctrines of Tendai). The boy soon called attention to the hard passages and began asking questions about them. The fact was that these were the very points on which, from ancient times, the scholars of the perfect religion (Tendai) had been in doubt, and had often controverted. Genkō said to himself—this is no common boy.

The Boy Becomes a Disciple of Kōen

As the boy was so much above the ordinary in natural talents, and his fame spread, Genkō thought himself entirely too dull and ignorant to be his teacher, and declared that the boy must study the profound principles of the perfect religion under the direction of a competent scholar. So on the eighth day of the fourth month in the third year of Kyūan (1147), he took him to become a disciple of Kōen, who was the head priest of the Kudokuin Temple on Mount Hiei. Kōen, a disciple of Hokkyō Kōkaku of Sugiu, and a man of no small prominence at the time, was regarded as one of the most distinguished men on Mount Hiei. Kōen was much surprised on hearing of the boy's extreme cleverness, and in his delight said, "Last night in a dream I saw the full moon coming into my room. It was surely a token that I was soon to meet one worthy of becoming a teacher of the Law."[1]

His Ordination to the Priesthood

On the eighth day of the eleventh month of that same year his beautiful locks were shaven off, and he donned the vestments of the Law. The ceremony of receiving the commandments of the Greater Vehicle[2] was performed in the Kaidan Hall.

His Early Desire for the Life of Retirement

One day he said to his teacher Kōen, "I have already become a priest, but I want truly to retire from the world into the solitude of the forest." In reply Kōen advised him as follows, "It is all right for you thus to wish for seclusion from the world, but before carrying out your purpose you should first read the sixty volumes." "The reason" said the boy, "why I make this request to become a hermit, is that I may abandon all hope of worldly fame or profit, and pursue the study and practical discipline of the Law of Buddha, free from all distraction." Recognizing, however, the propriety of his teacher's counsel, he began the reading of these books in the spring of his sixteenth year, and after three years, he had read through the whole of the three divisions of the sixty volumes of the Tendai Scriptures.

[1] Sanskrit: Dharma.

[2] The Commandments, or Perfect Precepts, constitute the basic governing rules of action for a Buddhist of the Mahāyāna school. See Glossary under Precepts (*Śila*) and Mahāyāna (Greater Vehicle).

Hōnen's tonsure

The Young Priest's Profound Insight

Being naturally endowed with an excellent understanding, the order and succession of the four doctrines and the five periods[3] stood out in his mind with all the clearness of objects reflected from a bright mirror, and the profound truth of the so-called "three aspects in the one consciousness"[4] shone within him like a jewel, so that in his explanations he could all but surpass his teachers. Kōen, in his growing admiration for the youth, kept encouraging him to devote himself more and more diligently to the study of the Way, telling him he ought yet to attain the rank of high priest. But he, on his part, never uttered a syllable to show that he had any such ambitions, but rather turned away from studies which might promote his worldly advancement and hastened to get away from a teacher who would instill such thoughts into his mind. So on the twelfth of the ninth month in the sixth year of Kyūan (1150) in his eighteenth year, he left Kōen and entered the fold of Jigembō Eikū at Kurodani in the western section of the mountain. He told Eikū that from the time he was a child to manhood, he never could forget his father's dying council and that was what deepened

[3] The doctrinal classification of the teachings of Shākyamuni (Japanese: Shaka) from the standpoint of the Tendai sect.

[4] A technical term, peculiar to the Tendai sect, for a meditation in which there is a simultaneous recognition of the aspects of reality—being, non-being, and the unity of both in a momentary act of consciousness.

his resolve to give himself up forever to a life of retirement from the world. Eikū was so delighted to find one so young utterly devoted to the pious life, that he said he was one of Nature's saints,[5] and gave him the nickname of Hōnembō (Nature's own priest), but his real name he made up of the first character in Genkō's name, and the second in Eikū's (his own), and so called him Genkū.

The Kurodani Temple, where once stood Hōnen's hermitage

[5] The original here used is *hōnen dōri no hijiri* which means a natural born saint. The word *hōnen* or *jinen* is quite common in Buddhist literature. Kōbō Daishi says in his *Sokushin Jōbutsugi*, "By *hōnen* I mean that all things are as they are according to their own nature, apart from outside influences."

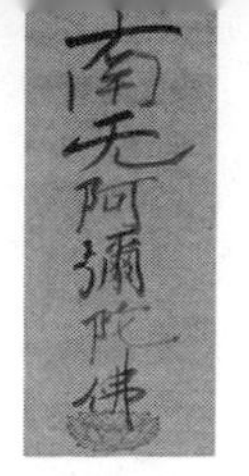

4. HŌNEN, THE ADMIRATION OF SCHOLARS

His Grasp of the Scriptures From the time of his entering the monastery at Kurodani he gave up all thought of worldly promotion, and applied his mind with all diligence to the seeking of salvation. And so, with the object of securing entire relief in the present life from the fated transmigration, he read through all the Sūtras and commentaries of the Tendai and other sects many times, hoping to find in some of them what he sought. So subtle were his natural powers, that he was able to penetrate with apparently little effort into the meaning and reason of them all.

Admiration of Scholars Hōnen was a man of such ready understanding that he thoroughly grasped the meaning of a work, however voluminous it was. He delved into the secret meaning of the doctrines of Buddhism, familiarizing himself with the general principles of the Eight Sects,[1] so that when he would meet an eminent scholar of any of the sects, he was always ready with his own exposition of their tenets, and he invariably won from them all their assent to his interpretations, together with words of high commendation for his acumen.

Hōnen's Discussion with Eikū on the Essence of the Precepts One day in his study of the original teachings of Tendai Daishi, the founder of the Tendai sect in China, the question arose as to what was the essence of the precepts in the perfect doctrine of the absolute reality. Jigembō maintained that everything depended upon the man's conscious soul activity, whereas Hōnen insisted that it was rather the operation upon his soul of that mysterious something which inevitably comes upon one in the ceremonial act of receiving the precepts. Their discussion went on for several hours, neither of them willing to yield to the other, till at last Jigembō became so angry that he struck Hōnen with a wooden pillow. At this Hōnen left the room. After Jigembō had reflected on the matter

[1] There were at the time of Hōnen eight officially recognized sects of Buddhism: 1) Kusha, 2) Jōjitsu, 3) Ritsu, 4) Hossō, 5) Sanron, 6) Kegon, 7) Tendai, 8) Shingon.

for some minutes, he went to Hōnen's room, and acknowledged that what Hōnen had said expressed the ultimate meaning of Tendai Daishi's teaching on the perfect precept of the "one reality." Thus we see that selfishness has no place in Buddhism, for Hōnen became the teacher, and his teacher turned pupil.

Hōnen in a Temple at Saga

An Earnest Seeker of Salvation

In the first year of Hōgen (1156), in his twenty-fourth year, he said good-bye to Eikū, and went to the Shōryōji Temple at Saga, where he spent seven days in earnest prayer to the Buddha, that he might be shown the true way of salvation. The image of Buddha in this temple was one which had been brought originally from India to China and thence to Japan, and was one of the most wonderful images in all three countries. It was not, therefore, without good reason that he went to such a temple to pour out his soul in prayer.

His Interview with Zōshun, the Famous Hossō Scholar

When he had finished the seven days of special prayer at Shōryōji, he went thence to Nara. Coming in the habit of a pilgrim, he had an interview with Zōshun Sōzu, a distinguished scholar of the Hossō sect, who later obtained the posthumous rank of *Sōjō* (bishop). Seeing Hōnen on the veranda of the temple, Zōshun opened the door and invited him in, and they at once began conversation about the Law which lasted several hours.

Hōnen asked him some questions about the doctrines of his sect, some of which he was not able to answer, when Hōnen would suggest explanations of his own. Zōshun was much surprised, and exclaimed, "Surely this is no common man, but an incarnation of some mighty Buddha. Even though I should meet that great patriarch of our sect himself, he would verily not surpass this man. No words can describe the depth and breadth of his wisdom." So saying, he forthwith became Hōnen's disciple, and continued so all his life, never failing to bring him some present every year. Hōnen is reported to have said, "Such is every good scholar. When he is convinced that he has found one worthy of being his master, he should become his follower."

Hōnen's visit to Zōshun

His Interview with Kwanga, the Famous Sanron Scholar

At Daigo there was a distinguished scholar of the Sanron sect, Gon-Risshi Kwanga. Thither Hōnen wended his way, and opened his mind to Kwanga. The latter was simply speechless. He went into an inner chamber and brought out some books encased in ten small boxes, saying "I know of no one worthy of being my successor to transmit these doctrines of my sect to posterity. You have already fully entered into their profoundest depths. I therefore hand over to you these books with all our secret doctrines." With such words of extravagant panegyric he passed them over to him. A priest called Ashōbō, also known as Shinshi Nyūdō, and several others who accompanied Hōnen, were filled with wonder and awe on seeing and hearing these things.

Hōnen on the Doctrinal Classification of the Sects

"It has always been the usage of each of the sects to classify the holy teachings of Buddha—this as comparatively profound and that as comparatively superficial—according to their several points of view, with all the Sūtras as grist for its own mill. The Tendai believes all the Scriptures teach Tendai doctrines, the Kegon, that they teach theirs, and so also with the Hossō and the Sanron, the Scriptures are all equally their own."

Hōnen's Criticism of Narrow Sectarianism

Hōnen was reported to have said, "The scholars of the different sects fail to comprehend that every sect has its own peculiar standpoint, and so as soon as they discover anything contrary to their own, they at once pronounce such teaching false. This is quite unreasonable. So long as each sect has its distinctive features, they cannot be expected to be all alike, and it is a matter of course that each should have something against every other."

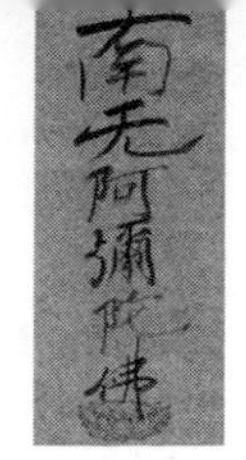

5. HŌNEN, THE FOUNDER OF THE JŌDO SECT

Hōnen's Discovery in the Scriptures

As Hōnen was well acquainted with the doctrines of the various sects of the Holy Path (*Shōdō*),[1] all the learned men of the Hossō and Sanron, as well as of the Tendai and Kegon sects, spoke in the highest terms of his marvelous understanding and extensive scholarship. Nevertheless he was still troubled about the way of attaining salvation, and ill at ease. So with a view to the discovery of the path leading thereto immediately after death, he read the whole of the Buddhist Scriptures[2] through five times. He dwelt long and intently upon every trace he could find of what Shaka[3] himself had taught during his lifetime, only to find one difficulty after another present-

Hōnen proclaiming the new Evangel

[1] See Glossary under Holy Path (*Shōdō*) for a description of the *Shōdō* path as seen by Hōnen.

[2] The collection of all the teachings and precepts which the historical Buddha taught during his whole lifetime, and the works of his disciples; in Sanskrit: *Tripitaka*.

[3] The Japanese word for Shākyamuni, the historical Buddha. See Glossary under Shaka.

ing itself to his mind. At last he found a book called *Ōjōyōshū*[4] written by Genshin, based upon a commentary by the venerable Zendō on the *Meditation Sūtra*. While perusing this book, it occurred to him to examine Zendō's commentary. He found that the writer earnestly inculcated the principle that by the practice of the *Nembutsu*, even the ordinary man, with all his heart distractions, may understand how he may be born into the Pure Land immediately at death, and thus the way of deliverance was made very easy.

This Leads to the Founding of the Sect

Though he had noticed it every time he turned over the pages of Scripture, he read this again three times with special attention, and finally came to the following passage: "Only repeat the name of Amida[5] with all your heart. Whether walking or standing, sitting or lying, never cease the practice of it even for a moment. This is the very work which unfailingly issues in salvation, for it is in accordance with the Original Vow of that Buddha."[6] Through this passage he was led to the conclusion that the common man, no matter how far removed from the age of the Buddha, may by the repetition of Amida's name, in virtue of that Buddha's Original Vow, of a certainty attain birth into the Pure Land. And so in the spring of the fifth year of Jōan (1175), when he was forty-three years of age, he unhesitatingly abandoned all other forms of religious discipline, and applied himself exclusively to the practice of the *Nembutsu*.

Meditation Compared with the *Nembutsu*

Hōnen once said, "to attain birth into the Pure Land, there is nothing better than calling upon the Buddha's name." In reply to this, Jigembō urged the superiority of meditation on the Buddha. Then Hōnen defended his position, by showing that the calling upon Amida's name was in accord with His Original Vow, but Jigembō insisted that his teacher, the deceased Ryōnin Shōnin, had held that meditation was better. To this Hōnen replied, "He was indeed born before us, but even so, what difference does that make?" At this Jigembō became very angry, but Hōnen continued, "Ac-

[4] "Collection [of Scriptural Passages] on the Essentials for Birth into Pure Land," written by the Tendai priest Genshin.

[5] The Buddha Amida, through whose Original Vow all men may be born into the Pure Land. See Glossary under Amida Buddha.

[6] Amida's vow that all sentient beings who call with faith upon his name shall be born into the Pure Land. See Glossary under Original Vow.

cording to Zendō, although the Buddha Shaka taught there was merit in the meditative and non-meditative good works, yet if we enquire into the final purpose of Amida's Original Vow, we find that it was to lead all sentient beings to the one practice of calling upon His name (*Nembutsu*). Thus it is perfectly evident, that the supreme place is given to the invoking of this Buddha, and all you need to do is to read the Scriptures over carefully to find this out."

Hōnen's Homes

Shortly after Hōnen began to devote himself exclusively to this one practice, he left his den in Kurodani on Mount Hiei, and removed to a place called Hirodani on the Western Mountain, and then after a little while, finding a quiet retreat in the neighborhood of Yoshimizu on the Eastern Mountain, he left Hirodani and settled there. When people visited him there, he explained the doctrines of the Jōdo (Pure Land), and urged upon them the practice of the *Nembutsu*. His influence increased daily, and the numbers converted to his *Nembutsu* sect grew like the clouds in the sky. Though he changed his residence quite often, moving to the Kawaraya at Kamo, to Komatsudono, the Kachiodera Temple, and to Ōtani, he never neglected his work of evangelism. His fame at length filled the Court, and his influence spread throughout the land. This is due to the fact, I think, that the teaching of the Amida Buddha has a special affinity for our country, and that the cult of the *Nembutsu* is peculiarly adapted to these latter degenerate days, when men have forsaken the Law. Ōtani is the place where Hōnen lived, died, and was buried, and where the building called Mieidō, containing his relics, now stands, evidencing by its small size of some thirty by one hundred feet the simplicity in which he lived.

Hōnen's Search for Salvation

Hōnen once said, "Having a deep desire to obtain salvation, and with faith in the teachings of the various Scriptures, I practice many salvation forms of self-discipline. There are indeed many doctrines in Buddhism, but they may all be summed up in the 'three learnings,' namely the precepts, meditation, and knowledge, as practiced by the adherents of the Lesser and Greater Vehicles,[7] and the exoteric and esoteric sects. But the fact is that I do not keep

[7] The two branches of Buddhism. The so-called Lesser Vehicle (Hīnayāna), and the so-called Greater Vehicle (Mahāyāna). See Glossary under Mahāyāna (Greater Vehicle) and Hīnayāna (Lesser Vehicle).

even one of the precepts, nor do I attain to any one of the many forms of meditation. A certain priest has said that without the observance of the *śila* (precepts), there is no such thing as the realization of *samādhi*.[8] Moreover the heart of the ordinary unenlightened man, because of his surroundings, is always liable to change, just like monkeys jumping from one branch to another. It is indeed in a state of confusion, easily moved, and with difficulty controlled. In what way does right and indefectible[9] knowledge arise? Without the sword of indefectible knowledge, how can one get free from the chains of evil passion, whence comes evil conduct? And unless one gets free from evil conduct and evil passions, how shall he obtain deliverance from the bondage of birth and death? Alas! What shall I do? What shall I do? The like of us are incompetent to practice the three disciplines of the precepts, meditation, and knowledge.

"And so I enquired of a great many learned men and priests whether there is any other way of salvation than these three disciplines, that is better suited to our poor abilities, but I found none who could either teach me the

[8] *Samādhi* here signifies a form of abstract meditation.

[9] Indefectible knowledge (Sanskrit: *anāsravajñāna*). The original here is *muro* (Sanskrit: *anāsrava*, indefectible). This expression is used in the opposite sense to *uro* (Sanskrit: *sāsrava*), which means literally "having a leak," i.e. having such an evil nature that its defects leak out through the five senses. It therefore means the state of complete exemption from such an evil nature and the evil consequences which flow from it.

Hōnen's discussion with scholars at Ōhara

way or even suggest it to me. At last I went into the Library at Kurodani on Mount Hiei, where all the Scriptures were, all by myself, and with a heavy heart, read them all through. While doing so, I hit upon a passage in Zendō's *Commentary on the Meditation Sūtra*, which runs as follows: 'Whether walking or standing, sitting or lying, only repeat the name of Amida with all your heart. Never cease the practice of it even for a moment. This is the very work which unfailingly issues in salvation, for it is in accordance with the Original Vow of that Buddha.' On reading this I was impressed with the fact, that even ignorant people like myself, by reverent meditation upon this passage, and an entire dependence upon the truth in it, never forgetting the repetition of Amida's sacred name, may lay the foundation for that good *karma*, which will with absolute certainty eventuate in birth into the blissful land."

Hōnen's Reason for Founding a Sect

Hōnen once said, "The reason I founded the Jōdo sect was that I might show the ordinary man how to be born into the Buddha's real land of compensation.[10] According to the Tendai sect, the ordinary man may be born into the so-called Pure Land, but that land is conceived of as a very inferior place. Although the Hossō sect conceives of it as indeed a very superior place, they do not allow that the common man can be born there at all.

[10] The Pure Land of Amida Buddha.

And all the sects, though differing in many points, all agree in not allowing that the common man can be born into the Buddha's land of real compensation; while, according to Zendō's *Commentary*, which laid the foundation of the Jōdo sect, it was made clear that birth into that land is possible even for the common man. But many said to me, 'You surely can promote the *Nembutsu* way of attaining *Ōjō*[11] without establishing a new sect. You are doing this merely out of ambition, to appear superior to others.' At first sight this seems quite plausible, but on further reflection it really misses the point. Unless I start a separate sect, the truth that the common man may be born into the Buddha's land of compensation will be obscured, and it will be hard to realize the deep meaning of Amida's Original Vow. I, therefore, in accordance with the interpretation given by Zendō, unhesitatingly proclaim the doctrine of the land of real compensation. This is by no means a question of personal ambition."

Hōnen's Doctrine a Message to His Age

Hōnen said to Shinjakubō, a priest from the province of Harima, "Suppose two Imperial orders were sent out, one for the western and one for the eastern provinces. What would you think, if the one intended for the western were by mistake taken to the eastern provinces, or vice versa? Would the people observe them?" After some thought Shinjakubō replied, "Even though they were Imperial orders, how would it be possible for the people to observe them?" "Right you are," said Hōnen. "Now by the two Imperial orders, I mean the teachings we inherit from Shaka belonging to the so-called three periods, that of the perfect Law, the imitation of the Law, and the ending of the Law.[12] The practice of the so-called Holy Path (*Shōdō*), belongs to the periods of the perfect Law and its imitation, and is only attainable by men of superior capacity and wisdom. Let us call this the Imperial order to the western provinces. The practice of the so-called Pure Land (*Jōdo*) belongs to the degenerate age when the Law has fallen into decay, in which even the most worthless may find the way of salvation. Let us liken this to the Imperial order to the eastern provinces. So it would never do to confuse these two paths, only one of which is suited to all three periods. I once discussed the doctrines of the Holy Path and of the Pure Land with several scholars at Ōhara, and admitted that they both are equally Buddhistic, just as both horns of an ox are equally his own. I went on to show that

[11] Birth in the Pure Land.

[12] For further details see Glossary under Three Periods of the Law.

from the standpoint of human capacity, my doctrine of the Pure Land is much superior and has had by far the greater success. Though the Holy Path is indeed profound, it belongs to an age already past, and is not suited to men of the present day; and while the Pure Land seems shallow it really is just the thing for our generation. When I thus won in the argument, the audience applauded, deeply convinced of the truth of the saying, 'In the period of the latter days of the Law, which last ten thousand years, all other Sūtras shall perish, but the one teaching of Amida alone shall remain to bless men and endure.'"

His Unceasing Practice of the *Nembutsu*

From the time Hōnen began to repeat the name seventy thousand times a day, he did nothing else day or night. And if anyone came to ask questions about religion, while he seemed to be listening to the questions, he lowered his voice, but really did not cease repeating the *Nembutsu* for a moment.

Hōnen Shōnin

II.

HŌNEN'S TEACHING ON THE WAY OF JŌDO

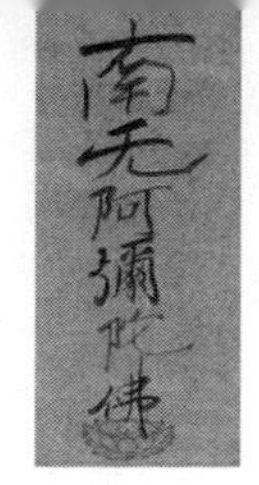

6. THINGS HŌNEN WAS ALWAYS SAYING (PART I)

The Need of Oral Teaching

"A man who reads about the doctrines of the Jōdo without receiving oral instruction will miss the thing really necessary to the attainment of *Ōjō*. Men of high station such as Nāgārjuna and Vasubandhu,[1] and on the other hand men of the lowest rank of common latter-day sinners guilty of the ten evil deeds and the five deadly sins,[2] used to be the object of the Buddha Shaka's exhortations to enter the Land of Perfect Bliss. Now we common men of the lowest class, when we hear the Buddha exhorting good men, at once begin to depreciate ourselves, and to think that we cannot be born into the Pure Land, and so we actually by our doubts prevent ourselves from reaching that birth after death. The main thing, then, is that we clearly distinguish between the teaching intended for the good, and that applicable to the evil like ourselves. If we are so minded, our faith in the certainty of our own birth will become assured, and through the power of the Buddha's Original Vow we shall accomplish our birth into that land at death."

Simple Invocation of the Name

"There is no secret about calling upon the sacred name except that we put our heart into the act, in the conviction that we shall be born into the Land of Perfect Bliss."

"Save me Amida Buddha!"

"We must not think that the expression *Namu Amida Butsu* means anything but simply 'Save me, oh! Amida Buddha.' So then let us pray in our hearts, 'Save me, oh Amida,' and say with our lips '*Namu Amida Butsu.*'"

[1] Indian born philosophers influential in the development of early Mahāyāna Buddhism.

[2] Of the five deadly sins there are two kinds, simple and compound. The simple ones are: 1) killing one's father, 2) killing one's mother, 3) killing an *Arhat* (one who has attained enlightenment), 4) wounding the Buddha's body, 5) breaking the friendship of a priest. The so-called compound sins are: 1) destroying temples, Scriptures, or images, 2) reviling the Buddha's laws, 3) persecuting a Buddhist priest, 4) committing any one of the five so-called deadly sins, 5) leading others to sin. The ten evil deeds are (A) Three physical: 1) killing, 2) stealing, 3) committing adultery; (B) Four of speech: 1) lying, 2) immoral language, 3) equivocation, 4) slandering; (C) Three in thought: 1) coveting, 2) anger, 3) wrong ideas.

The Vilest May be Saved

"While believing that even a man guilty of the ten evil deeds and the five deadly sins may be born into the Pure Land, let us, as far as we are concerned, not commit even the smallest sins. If this is true of the wicked, how much more of the good. We ought to continue the practice of the *Nembutsu* uninterruptedly, in the belief that ten repetitions, or even one, will not be in vain.[3] If this is true of merely one repetition, how much more of many!"

The Buddha flanked by the Bodhisattvas Kwannon and Seishi

[3] The Buddha Amida vowed that if, with faith, one repeats His name ten times, or even once, this shall result in birth in the Pure Land.

Faith and Works Go Hand in Hand

"If a man says he can be born by ten repetitions of the sacred name, or even one, and then begins to be careless about the practice, his faith will hinder his practice. On the other hand if a man says, as Zendō did, that he unceasingly repeats the *Nembutsu*, but in his heart has doubts about the certainty of *Ōjō*, in the case of one who only practices it once, then his practice will hinder his faith. So then, believe that you can attain *Ōjō* by one repetition, and yet go on practicing it your whole life long. If you think there is uncertainty as to the efficacy of calling upon the sacred name once, it means that there is doubt about it every time you call upon the sacred name. The Buddha's Vow was to give birth into the Pure Land to those who would call upon His name even once, and so there is efficacy in every repetition of the sacred name."

Invoke with Heart and Voice Together

"Do not be worrying as to whether your evil passions are strong or otherwise, or whether your sins are light or heavy. Only invoke Amida's name with your lips, and let the conviction accompany the sound of your voice, that you will of a certainty be born into the Pure Land."

***Nembutsu* the Main Thing**

"Even though you may be doing something else, let that be done while you go on with the main work of life, which consists in the practice of the *Nembutsu*, and do not let it be a sort of side work to anything else."

It Means Hating the World

"The countenance of a man who longs for Paradise, and fixes his whole mind upon the one object of reaching it, will always appear as if he had a hatred and abhorrence of the world."

Its Peculiarity Is No Peculiarity

"The peculiarity of the *Nembutsu* is absence of peculiarity, and the only thing is to believe the Buddha's word, and practice the *Nembutsu*, and you will surely be born into the Pure Land."

At Meal Time Too

"Sometimes a man dies from being choked by his food when taking a meal. Now I say, call upon the sacred name every time that you chew your food and swallow it."

***Nembutsu* and the Nature of Things**

"We speak of the reason of things. For example, a flame of fire rises towards the sky; water flows downwards; some fruits are sour, others sweet. These are simple facts in the natural world. Now there is no doubt at all that we have facts equally in keeping with the nature of things, when we speak of the Buddha's Vow, in which He took an oath to guide all simple sentient beings, who do nothing but earnestly call upon His name, and welcome them into His Paradise."

Amida's Great Vow

"When Zendō speaks of the all-comprehensive Vow, as it is explained in the *Larger Sūtra*,[4] he means that by virtue of Amida's great Vow, His meritorious *karma*, and His mighty power, all ordinary mortals, whether good or bad, may every one attain birth into the Pure Land. An incapable man like me can only put his entire trust in the great Vow."

Saves Even the Foolish Hōnen

"I am a man who wears no official head-dress. I am nothing but the foolish Hōnen, weighed down by the ten evils, and I say that the only way for me to attain *Ōjō* is by calling upon the sacred name."

The Danger of Learning

"If one becomes a learned man, there is danger of his losing the disposition to practice the *Nembutsu*."

Depend Only on the *Nembutsu*

"Let the *Nembutsu* of the Original Vow stand by itself and receive help from no other quarter. By outside help I mean that of one's own wisdom, the observance of the commandments (*sīla*), religious aspiration, deeds of charity, and the like. But the good man, as he is, and the bad man too, as he is, each in his own natural condition, should seek help nowhere except in the *Nembutsu*. But he is in harmony with the mind of the Buddha who practices it by giving up his wickedness and becoming good. A man who cannot make up his mind, but is always thinking himself unfit in this way or that, will not be sure of attaining birth into the Pure Land."

[4] The Sūtra on the Buddha of Infinite Life. See Glossary under *Larger Sūtra*.

Shaka's Charge to Ānanda "It is written in the Sūtra that Shaka said to Ānanda,[5] 'Preserve well these words. I mean preserve well the name of the Buddha of Endless Life (Amitāyus).'[6] A man may hear of the sacred name, but unless he believes, he is just like one who has not heard. And though he may say he believes, unless he calls upon the sacred name, he is just the same as an unbeliever. So the only thing is always to be calling upon the sacred name."

The Failure of Meditation "Let devotees of the present day give up their so-called meditations as if they were required by the Law. Even though a man would meditate upon the images of the Buddhas and Bodhisattvas in Paradise, the fact is he is incapable of picturing to himself the Buddhas as represented in the images made by such famous sculptors as Unkei and Kōkei. Even though he tries to meditate upon the things which beautify the Land of Bliss, he finds it hard even to picture to his mind the beauties of the flowers and fruit of the cherry, plum, and peach of this world with which he is so familiar. So simply believe the words in Zendō's *Commentary*, which says, 'That Buddha is now present in the Land of Bliss, having already attained enlightenment. All ye sentient beings ought to know that His great Original Vow was not in vain, and that if you call upon His name you shall without fail be born into the Pure Land. Put your whole trust in that Original Vow and call upon His name with all your heart.'"

When Is *Ōjō Karma* Complete? "The completion of the *karma* necessary for birth into the Pure Land, may be at any ordinary time, or at the time of death. There is no distinction made between the two in the language of the Original Vow."

How to Embark on the Ship of the Original Vow "There are two conditions of embarking on the ship of the Original Vow, and also two ways of not doing so. Of the two conditions in which a man does not embark, one is when he commits sin. The reason of this is that if he sins, though he practices the *Nembutsu*, he thinks he will not be born into the Pure Land, and so he does not embark.

[5] The favorite disciple of the Buddha.

[6] One of several terms for Amida Buddha. See Glossary under Amida Buddha.

The second case of failure is when a man's mind goes out in aspiration after enlightenment. And the reason is that even though he does say the *Nembutsu*, he thinks he will be born into the Pure Land because he says the *Nembutsu* under the impulse of this aspiration, and that without that impulse the *Nembutsu* will be of no avail. Whereas the fact is, that because he puts this aspiration first, and the Original Vow second, he fails to embark. Now on the other hand, in regard to those two conditions of really embarking, I would say, that the first is in the case of a man who commits sin. And what I mean is that such a man, when he sins, is sure that he is going to fall into hell, but at once calls upon the sacred name of the Original Vow, and he is overwhelmed with delight at the thought that he will assuredly be born into the Pure Land, the result being that he is so born. Secondly a man embarks who aspires after enlightenment. Now from the remote past, he has had this aspiration, and yet he has not thereby been freed from the bondage of birth and death, and so, quite apart from the possession or otherwise of religious aspiration, and also irrespective of the gravity or otherwise of his sinfulness, he attains to birth into the Pure Land by simply calling continually upon the sacred name. It is when we come to think thus, that we embark upon the ship of the Original Vow, depending upon the Buddha's power and that alone."

Hōnen attains *Samādhi*

Singleness of Purpose "When a deer is being pursued by the hunters, it does not stop even to look around for its fellows or look back at its pursuers, but with all eagerness, hastens straight forward, and no matter how many may be following, it escapes in safety. It is with the same determination that a man fully entrusts himself to the Buddha's power, and without regard to anything else, steadfastly sets his mind upon being born into the Pure Land."

Intense Earnestness "When a man is calling upon the sacred name he ought to do it with the earnestness of the man in dire distress who is crying 'Oh save me now.'"

Believe You Have Already Received "Where one is to receive something from another, which is better, to have already received, or not yet to have received? I, Genkū,[7] repeat the *Nembutsu* as if I had already received."

[7] The name given to him by his teacher, Jigembō Eikū; Hōnen uses it here to refer to himself with humility.

Certainty of *Ōjō*

"Birth into the Pure Land is certain, when you think it so, but also uncertain when you think it so."

To Jump Ten Feet, Jump Fifteen

"A man who plans to jump over a moat ten feet wide, must bend every effort to jump fifteen feet. And so a man who would be born into the Pure Land must concentrate his energy upon believing that he will of a certainty be so born."

Whatever Befalls, Free from All Care

"In life I pile up merit by the practice of the *Nembutsu*, and at death I go to the Pure Land. Whatever befalls, I have made up my mind not to be anxious about myself, and so, come life, come death, nothing troubles me."

If Only I Had but Attained

Once when Hōnen remarked, "If only I had but attained!" Jōgwambō heard it and said, "Well, if even a man like you feels uncertain about your future, what will become of the rest of us?" Whereupon Hōnen laughed heartily, and said, "Until a man is truly sitting upon the lotus stand in the Pure Land, how is it possible for him to be entirely free from such thoughts?"

***Ōjō* Possible for Everyone**

When someone once said to Hōnen that his repetition of the *Nembutsu* must be very acceptable to the Buddha, he asked "Why?" "Because you are a wise man, and know in detail what merit there is in the repetition of the sacred name, clearly understanding the meaning of the Buddha's Original Vow." At this Hōnen replied, "You have not yet really come to believe in the Original Vow at all. As to calling upon the sacred name of the Original Vow of the Buddha Amida, it makes no difference whether the man be a wood-cutter, a gatherer of grass or greens, or a drawer of water or the like, whether he be utterly unlettered in Buddhism or other religions, it makes no difference, I say, so long as he calls upon the sacred name. If he believes his *Ōjō* is certain, and with all sincerity makes his petition, and keeps repeating the *Nembutsu*, he is the very best kind of believer. If it is possible by wisdom to get free from the bondage of life and death, why indeed should I, Genkū, have given up the Holy Path (*Shōdō-mon*) and devoted myself exclusively to this Pure Land doctrine (*Jōdo-mon*)?"

The Buddha Amida

Ōjō Has Nothing to Do with Fish-eating

Some people were conversing about the future life, some saying that fish-eaters will be born into the Pure Land, others that they will not. Hōnen overhearing them said, "If it is a case of eating fish, cormorants would be born into the Pure Land; and if it is a case of not eating them, monkeys would be so born. But I am sure that whether a man eats fish or not, if he only calls upon the sacred name, he will be born into the Pure Land."

In Your Devotion to Amida Despise Not Other Buddhas

Once when Hōnen was teaching the *Nembutsu* devotees some things they ought to observe, he said, "You should not say, as some do, that because you put your trust in Amida and believe in the *Nembutsu*, it is all right to have nothing to do with the merciful vows of the many Buddhas and Bodhisattvas. Even though you may believe in the Amida Buddha, your faith is quite one-sided if you despise the many Buddhas, or doubt Shaka's holy teachings. If your faith is not right, it is not in harmony with the mind of the Buddha Amida, and it is certain His merciful Vow has nothing to do with you."

The Buddha Shaka

Antinomianism

"There are those who say that the effort to avoid sin and improve oneself is making light of Amida's Vow, and the frequent repetition of the *Nembutsu*, and the effort to pile up a large number of them is equivalent to doubting his saving power, and many such like things one sometimes hears. But do not for a moment be misled by such misconceptions. Is there any place in any of the Sūtras where Amida encourages men to sin? Certainly not. Such things come from those who make no effort to get away from their own evil deeds, and who go on in their former sinful life. By such utterly unreasonable and false sayings, they would mislead ignorant men and women, urging them forward in the committing of sin and stirring up their evil passions within them. Now such persons are nothing less than a company of devils, and their work heathenish, and you ought to think of them as enemies to your reaching birth into that Pure Land of Perfect Bliss. Again, to say that frequent repetitions of the sacred name mean the encouragement of the principle of self-effort, shows utter ignorance of facts and is a deplorable blunder."

Jiriki, Self-Power, and _Tariki_, Other-Power, Defined

"Even one repetition or two of the sacred name must be said to be the *Nembutsu* of salvation by one's own power, if one does it with that thought in his heart; while a hundred or a thousand repetitions day and night for a hundred or a thousand days, so long as one does it with an entire trust in the merits of the great Vow, looking up in confidence to Amida with every repetition, constitute the *Nembutsu* of salvation by Amida's power alone."[8]

Special _Nembutsu_ Practice

"We ought often to arrange special times for the repetition of the *Nembutsu*, and stimulate both mind and body in its practice. There is a tendency with us, when our eyes or ears become accustomed to anything, gradually to lose interest in it, and with our daily avocations morning and night pressing us, we are in danger of abbreviating our religious duties. So in order to keep our spirits active, we should do well to fix upon certain special times for the practice of the *Nembutsu*. And you ought to beautify the room where you practice it, and adorn it with floral offerings and incense, according as your circumstances permit, and when you go into the room, you should purify your bodies and repeat the *Nembutsu* either six or twelve hours a day. Where several do it together, you should enter the room by turns, only keeping up the practice without cessation, and this as the circumstances of each severally permit. By thus arranging so as to suit everyone's convenience, these special services may always be held for seven days at a time."

[8] See Glossary under Other-Power (*Tariki*) and Self-Power (*Jiriki*).

How to Get Ready for Death "May it be that when you come down to the closing scene of life, you shall, with a composed mind, look into the face of Amida Buddha, call upon His name with your lips, and in your heart be able to await with confidence the welcome to be extended to you by His holy retinue. Even though through the days and years of life, you have piled up much merit by the practice of the *Nembutsu*, if at the time of death you come under the spell of some evil, and at the end give way to an evil heart, and lose the power of faith in and practice of the *Nembutsu*, it means that you lose that birth into the Pure Land immediately after death. This is why Zendō so tenderly urged us to pray thus: 'May we, the disciples of the Buddha, when we come to die, suffer no mental perversion, nor come under the spell of any hallucination, nor lose the consciousness of the truth, but, free from agony of mind and body, may we in peace of mind, like those in an ecstasy, have that holy retinue of Amida come to meet us, and, embarking safely on the ship of his Original Vow, may we have our birth into Amida Buddha's Pure Land, and sit upon the lotus of the first rank.' From this it is clearer still that we should pray for a composed mind when death comes."

Keep Repeating the *Nembutsu* "The one way to be sure of reaching birth into the Pure Land is to be always repeating the *Nembutsu*. These are Zendō's own words: 'From the time that one has religious aspiration awakened within him right down to the end of life, he vows never to go back, but makes the Pure Land alone his sole objective.' 'Only repeat the name of Amida with all your heart, whether walking or standing, sitting or lying. Never cease the practice of it even for a moment. This is the very work which unfailingly issues in salvation, for it is in accordance with the Original Vow of that Buddha.'"

No Place for Pride "And now, if with all seriousness you believe in the *Nembutsu*, and truly become a *Nembutsu* devotee, as you look at other men, be very careful that you do not say within yourself, 'these fellows are far below me, and very much worse than I am. I am indeed a fine specimen of *Nembutsu* devotee, and far ahead of everyone else.' This is a wide world with many people in it, and even in the mountains or the depths of the forest there may be many splendid devotees of the *Nembutsu* that you know nothing whatever about, and so it is very wrong to be saying, 'there is none like me.' This is indeed nothing but pride. It is from occasions like this, that evil spirits come and hinder one from being born into the Pure Land. If indeed it were really so that I am thus superior, and all my sin destroyed by my own exertions, and I fit to go to the Pure Land, it would be all right. But the fact is that it is only through the power and merit of Amida's Vow, that I escape from evil passion and throw off my sins, and it is only because He Himself comes for us, to bring us to that Pure Land, that we are able to get there at all. If indeed, it were by my own power that I attained it, there might be some excuse for my pride. But wherever pride arises within the heart, it shows positively that we are in the wrong, both in our faith and practice, and are utterly out of harmony with the Vow of Amida Buddha, and neither He nor any of the Buddhas will extend us their protection. Yes, indeed beware!"

7. THINGS HŌNEN WAS ALWAYS SAYING (PART II)

A Warning to Hypocrites

"Now the fact is that you and I have so long been accustomed to look well upon this world, which in reality it hardly needs to be said is all a dream, that when we succeed in casting aside worldly fame and gain even in the smallest degree, we think we have done a wonderful thing, and so we feign disgust of the world. Shallow-minded people, not knowing our hearts, suppose we have done a great thing worthy of much admiration, and we, in self-satisfaction proceed to get away from the neighborhood of the metropolis, and hunt us out a small obscure dwelling in some lonely spot, while in reality we give a quite secondary place to attaining soul-peace, thinking only of appearing to men so forlorn as to awaken their compassion toward us. For example, we plant miserable looking flowers in the hedges around the temple buildings which enshrine the image of the Buddha, all of which are also made to look correspondingly poor and meager, while all the time we are thinking only of how we may win the applause and escape the censure of our fellow-men. The result therefore must be, that, going on in this way, with not the least thought or mention of such a thing as trusting in the Buddha's Vow, or praying for birth into the Pure Land, there is an utter absence of a 'most sincere heart,' and with it a complete failure to attain birth into the Pure Land. But by saying this, I do not mean that it does not matter at all how men look upon us, or that we should pay no attention whatever to the world's criticism of us, for we certainly should. But it would be too bad, I repeat, for us to be thinking of only outward appearances, and thereby be hindered in our efforts to attain *Ōjō*. It is for your sake that I direct your thoughts to these things."

Other Roads to *Ōjō* Besides the *Nembutsu*

"What is meant when we speak of religious discipline is simply the repetition of the *Nembutsu*. In reference to those other religious practices tending to the Land of Bliss, one should not let his heart wander hither and thither, but, while performing any one of them, keep his mind fixed upon it alone. Whether we consider the Vow of Amida, the preaching of Shaka, the exposition of Zendō, or the opinions of many other teachers, the *Nembutsu*, according to them all, is the essential thing in the religious discipline which leads to birth into the Land of Bliss. As to other disciplines, none of them gives any particular instructions at all. Nevertheless, if there should be anyone, who has been learning the sacred Scriptures, and on that account finds it difficult to believe in the *Nembutsu*, let him bear in mind that everything else which he does, under whatever circumstances, according to other forms of religious discipline is all right, so long as he makes it an occasion for directing his thought and prayer to Amida and to his Land of Bliss, because such acts done in this spirit, may become the means of helping him to *Ōjō*."

Relation of the *Karma* of Prior States of Existence to *Ōjō*

"People say that a man can attain *Ōjō* by virtue of merit acquired in a previous state of existence. And there is no mistake about it, for through the sin or merit of a former life, men may be born to good or evil in this fleeting world. And if that be so, how much more must a great boon like *Ōjō* be influenced by the good done in a former existence. At least so it seems from the sacred Scriptures, and yet on the other hand they seem to teach that the attainment of *Ōjō* by the *Nembutsu* is quite independent of the good done in a former life. For example, it would appear from the *Meditation Sūtra* that even as wicked a criminal as one who murders his father and mother, or sheds the blood of a Buddha, may at death by but ten repetitions of the *Nembutsu* attain *Ōjō*. But those who have a large stock of merit from a former state, even without any special instruction, have a fear of evil, and their hearts yearn for the way of the Buddhas. So it is out of the question for them to be guilty of the five deadly sins. For this reason, when men guilty of them attain *Ōjō* by but ten repetitions, it is plain that it is not due to the merit they acquired in a former state.

"For in one of the Sūtras we read, to our comfort, 'Even though a man may have committed many sins, such as the five deadly ones, if he but hear the name with the six mystic characters *Na-mu-a-mi-da-butsu*, the chariot of fire (coming from hell to convey the sinner thither) will of itself disappear, and instead, a lotus stand will be brought (to take them to the Western Paradise), and the vilest sinners, even if they resort to no other means of salvation than that of calling upon Amida's name, shall be born into the Land of Perfect Bliss. And though the obstruction of their *karma* should be of the gravest kind, and they have no good *karma* to give them affinity for the Pure Land, if they will only entrust themselves to the power inherent in Amida's great Vow, they shall certainly be born into the Peaceful Land of Bliss.'"

How Hōzō Biku Became Amida Buddha

"If 'ordinary people,' sunk in the river of birth and death, are ever to get free from the fated transmigratory round and enter the way of the Buddhas, they must have awakened within them an aspiration after enlightenment, get rid of their evil passions by the severest austerities, practiced through innumerable ages of time. Now by so doing one may indeed become a Buddha, but for ordinary mortals, living in a world of five corruptions[1] like this, it is out of the question for them by their own power either to make vows or practice the disciplines necessary to Buddhahood. So they must wander about through the four modes of birth in the transmigratory states.[2] Now Amida Nyorai,[3] moved with sorrow at these things, away back in the distant past, when he was called Hōzō Biku, underwent the most trying austerities through innumerable *kalpas* of time,[4] during which he accumulated great merit, and thus became the Amida Buddha. He put into

[1] Characteristics of the world during and since Shaka's time: corruption of 1) time, 2) thought, 3) feeling, 4) person, and 5) life.

[2] The four modes of entering the course of transmigration: 1) birth from the womb, as animals, 2) birth from the egg, as birds, 3) from moisture, as fish and insects, 4) sudden birth without any apparent cause, as Bodhisattvas.

[3] Used as an honorific, Nyorai—"One thus come (to save all beings)"—is the Japanese rendering of the Sanskrit, *Tathāgata*.

[4] A general term designating an innumerable period of time. See Glossary under *Kalpa*.

Hōnen meets Zendō in a dream

the three letters of His name all the merit of the inner virtues of the four wisdoms, the three bodies, the ten faculties, and four fearlessnesses,[5] which inhere in every Buddha, together with all those external activities, such as the signs of eminence, light rays, sermons, practical service for others, and the like, and vowed that He would come from Paradise to welcome everyone who called upon His name ten times or even once, and that He would refuse to become a Buddha in case He failed to do this. Now He did become a Buddha, and is at this very moment present and alive in the world. And there is no doubt whatever, that every sentient being that calls upon His name shall assuredly attain *Ōjō*, just as Zendō says. Now I call him a real believer in the so-called 'Other-Power' (*Tariki*), who deeply believes the foregoing, and neither neglects the practice of the *Nembutsu*, nor doubts his own *Ōjō*."

(a) The Meaning of Tariki *Illustrated*

"We have many cases of this 'Other-Power' principle even in ordinary worldly matters. For example, if a man without feet, or with broken thighs, wishes to go on a long journey, seeing that he cannot do it himself, he rides

[5] The true nature or attributes of the Buddha's personality are inexpressible by human words and transcend thought, but if we give no explanation of them at all, we cannot make him our ideal or savior. If he be observed from the standpoint of his mental faculties, the Buddha has four wisdoms. His bodily form is threefold. With regard to his activities he is said to be endowed with ten powers and four fearlessnesses.

in a boat or some vehicle and does it easily. This is not by his own power, but by the power of another. If this is true of vehicles made by crooked-hearted people, who form the mass of the inhabitants of this wicked world, how much the less should we have any doubts about our being able to pass safely over the sea of birth and death, if we only get aboard that 'Other-Power' ship of the Original Vow, which Amida took five *kalpas* to make. Again there is a mysterious power in herbs to heal disease, in the magnet to attract iron, in the musk to produce a fragrant odor, and in the horn of the rhinoceros to keep water from sticking to its surface. This is all true of vegetables and animals that are without minds, and that make no vows, which nevertheless possess such wonderful power. Must there not then be a still more mysterious and mighty power in the Law of the Buddhas? There is power enough in the *Nembutsu*, even if pronounced but once, to destroy all the sins whose effects have persisted through eighty billions of *kalpas*. And so you ought to bear in mind that Amida has the power to come forth to welcome to His land those oppressed by the very worst *karma*, and you ought to believe that by simply calling upon His name you will be born there, quite irrespective of whether you have merit inherited from former lives or not, and no matter whether your sins be light or heavy. It is His promise that He will come forth from His paradise to welcome thither all, no matter whether they have broken the Law or kept it, whether they be rich or poor, high or low, if only they but call upon His name, and thus have their natures changed as if from tiles or stones into gold."

Repeat the *Nembutsu* Audibly

"A man would be very idle who would not even move his tongue when telling the beads on the rosary. Zendō, when explaining one of the three relationships which exist between men and Buddha, called the 'intimate relationship,' said: 'When a sentient being worships the Buddha, the Buddha sees him. When men call upon Him, He hears them. When they think upon Him, He thinks upon them. And so the three forms of action (words, deeds, and thoughts) of the Amida Buddha and of the devotees become one, like the intimacy of parents and children, and for this reason it is called the intimate relation.' Accordingly if you have a rosary in your hand, the Buddha will see it. If then you think in your heart 'now I am repeating the *Nembutsu*,' the Buddha has His mind upon you, and therefore you are in the happy condition of those whom He sees and cares for. Nevertheless you ought at least to move your tongue in prayer, so that your three forms of action will accord with those of the Buddha. I mean by the three forms of action, those of the body, the mouth, and the heart. And you must remember that the voice is an essential element in calling upon the sacred name in harmony with the Original Vow. And by a loud voice, I mean one loud enough for you to hear with your own ears."

Repeat the *Nembutsu* Even During Conversation

"Silence is excellent, but it is wrong to suppose that there is less merit in repeating the *Nembutsu* while talking to others than when silent. The *Nembutsu* is compared to gold, which, when burned in the fire, only has its color improved, and receives no injury though thrown into the water. In the same way the *Nembutsu*, though said when evil passions arise, is not defiled, nor does it lose its value though said when you are in conversation with others. If you bear this in mind, it is all right to increase the number of *Nembutsu* repetitions at your discretion. If when you are in the act of talking to someone, you should all of a sudden bethink yourself, 'Alas the *Nembutsu* I was just saying is all to no purpose,' do not allow yourself so to think for a moment. It matters not how you say it, for there is enough *karma* in it to result in *Ōjō*."

The Escaped Prisoner and Amida's Wonderful Ship

"You say you have no doubts about the Original Vow, and that you wish to go to the Land of Perfect Bliss, but that, though knowing that one may certainly attain *Ōjō*, you do not have an all-absorbing desire morning and night to get there as quickly as possible. This I say is very wrong of you. It is explained in the Sūtra, that one who has heard of the doctrine of the Pure Land, but is like one who has not heard, has barely escaped from these three evil worlds,[6] and is not yet rid of his sins. So I think that such a one's detestation of this world is still very superficial. Suppose for example, there is a man who has no mind to go down from the capital to one of the western provinces and someone offers him a boat. Although he may have no doubt that a boat will float upon the water, yet seeing he does not think he has any need of one, he will not be specially grateful for the offer.

"Suppose again the case of a man long in prison in his enemy's castle, who at last manages to escape. As he goes along the road he comes to a wide river or to the sea, and he cannot possibly cross either. Now if at such a crisis, his father, having gotten a boat ready beforehand, comes out to meet

[6] 1) hell, 2) the realm of hungry ghosts, 3) animality, which can be interpreted also as states of mind. See Glossary under Three Evil States.

him, his joy will surely know no bounds. In like manner, when we are bound hand and foot by such enemies as covetousness, anger, and evil passion, and shut up in the burning prison-house of the three worlds, if Amida, with all the deep sympathy of a compassionate mother, should come with the sharp sword of His sacred name, and cut the cords of birth and death with which we are fettered, should float the wonderful ship of His Original Vow upon the waves of our sea of sorrow, and bring us safely to the other shore, our tears of joy would flow like rivers, and unbounded indeed would be the thankfulness in our hearts. I would pity the man so insensate as not to have the very hairs of his head stand on end when contemplating such a deliverance. A man learns how to sin without having anyone teach him. In fact from the beginning until now, while passing through the transmigratory rounds, although in outer form we change, yet in heart we are the same, and so in all sorts of ways we have learned the art of sinning, and go on sinning without any compunction. When therefore we begin the practice of the *Nembutsu*, and hope thereby to attain *Ōjō*, seeing that this is the first mode of existence in which we have heard of such a thing, we find it hard all at once to exercise faith. Besides, men's hearts may be classified into two, viz., those of quick and those of dull faculties. The former readily come to understand and the latter only after long and painful effort. They are like men going to visit a sacred place. The swift-footed man gets there in a few hours, while the slow man takes the whole day for it and gets there by dark. If only they have the mind to go, they both will accomplish the same object. Thus if you are so minded and keep desiring it, you will in the course of time find that your faith becomes deeper and deeper."

The Very Easiest Way to *Ōjō*

"There are various kinds of *Nembutsu*, but the one which I advocate—repeating the six mystical characters—may be said to include all the other religious disciplines. The only thing is to put one's heartfelt trust in the Original Vow, repeat the sacred name with one's lips, and tell the rosary with one's fingers. It is the keeping of one's mind continually fixed thereon which constitutes the *karma* resulting in certain *Ōjō*. Seeing that the practice may be carried on, whether walking, standing, sitting, or lying, whensoever or wheresoever one may be, quite irrespective of whether one is impure in himself or in his speech, the *Nembutsu* is called an easy practice. Only remember that the first thing of all is to do it with a pure heart, and thus to exhort others to do it. You will then find that by degrees your heart will become purer and purer."

The Buddha Amida

What if My Nature Is Bad?

"Do not be troubled about whether your heart is good or bad, or your sin light or grievous. Only determine in your heart that you will be born into the Pure Land, and so repeat thc '*Namu Amida Butsu*' with your lips, and let the conviction accompany the sound of your voice, that you will of a certainty be born into the Pure Land. Then, according to your determined faith, that *karma* will certainly be produced which will result in your birth into that land."

Hōnen's Gracious Instruction to Women

Once some refined nuns and lay women went to Hōnen's house at Yoshimizu, and asked him whether it was true that sinful women could, by simply repeating the *Nembutsu*, attain the bliss of the Pure Land. He at once graciously explained that Amida had mercifully made a special Vow providing for women's birth into the Pure Land, and that surely they ought to be grateful for such compassion. On hearing this, it is said that they all shed tears of joy, and became devotees of the *Nembutsu.*

Let Not Your Faith be Disturbed, Not Even by a Buddha

"When Zendō says not to be disturbed in your faith by those whose thought and practice are different from yours, he means that just because someone of different religious ideas and practices has spoken to you something that seems good, you are not to abandon the *Nembutsu* nor indulge any doubts about the *Ōjō*. Even though a Buddha with an aureole of light about his head should come and stretch out his tongue and say, 'The thing is absurd that a common mortal full of evil passions and sins can be certain of *Ōjō* merely by repeating the *Nembutsu*; do not believe it,' even in such a case, I say, give no place to a single thought of doubt.

"I venture to say this, because in fact the whole of the Buddhas with one mind are engaged in leading all sentient beings to salvation. First of all Amida Nyorai made a Vow and said, 'If, after I attain Buddhahood, all the sentient beings in the ten quarters desire to be born into my land, and call upon my name as many as ten times, in dependence upon the virtue of my Vow, and still they should not so be born, I shall not accept of perfect enlightenment.' Now this Vow has been fulfilled. He did become a Buddha, and the Buddha Shaka came into the world to expound this Vow. Again at this time the multitudes of Buddhas in the six quarters,[7] innumerable as the sands of the Ganges, stretched forth their guileless tongues, till they covered

[7] These six include the four points of the compass, and in addition the worlds above and below this one. Also referred to as the "ten quarters." The number ten is merely used as a more complete characterization, including all intermediate points.

the great chiliocosm,[8] and testified that there was no doubt about the truth of what the Buddha Shaka had said in praise of the Original Vow of Amida, and of his exhortation to all sentient beings to the effect, that if they would but call upon that Buddha's sacred name they would be certain of *Ōjō*, and so they should believe his word. Thus all the Buddhas without exception, with one accord, unite in exhorting all common mortals with a view to their infallibly attaining *Ōjō*, one (Amida) making the Vow, another (Shaka) explaining it, and the others confirming it. Can it be that any Buddha would come and say such a thing as that they may not so be born? Nay indeed. But even if, for the sake of argument, we should assume that Buddhas did so come, Zendō says, you are not even then to be disturbed. How much less in case a Bodhisattva or a common mortal should come with such a message. If then you are so minded, it matters not even after you have heard the teaching about the *Nembutsu Ōjō*, and have begun the life of faith, whether anyone, whoever he may be, said such a thing, you are not to yield for a moment to thoughts of doubt. This is what we mean by a deep heart."

A Religious Adviser at Death-bed

"It is said by some, and there seems some force in it, that even though one is in the habit of saying the *Nembutsu*, if, when he draws near the end of life, he is unable to converse with his religious teacher, it would be hard for him to attain *Ōjō*. And again when one is very sick and his mind disturbed, it would be similarly hard. But according to Zendō, when a man who has made up his mind to go to the Land of Bliss and repeats the *Nembutsu*, whether many times or few, comes to die, the Amida Buddha with His retinue does come forth to meet him. So in the case of one who makes this his daily practice, even if there be no religious teacher near when he is on his death-bed, the Buddha will welcome him to that Land."

Mental Composure in the Death Agony

"It is a good thing for a man to pray that his last sickness may be as free from pain as possible. There are cases of men's dying without any sickness at all, and such are indeed beautiful. But the human body, made up of some eighty thousand particles of sinful dust, from which issue innumerable disorders, is liable to suffer the pains of a death-agony, as excruciating as if one were pierced through and through by hundreds of thou-

[8] Or "The Thousand Worlds." The English word *chiliocosm* is from the Greek *chilioi*, thousand plus *kosmos*, world.

sands of swords and spears. Having eyes, he is like one having none, trying in vain to see; and his tongue stiffens so that he cannot say what he would. This is one of the eight pains[9] mortals suffer, the bitter pain of death. And so even the devotee who believes in the Original Vow and prays for *Ōjō* is unable to escape it. And yet even though he becomes insensible through his agony, when he comes to draw his last breath, he is, by the power of the Amida Buddha, kept in his right mind and attains *Ōjō*. The moment of death is no longer than the time it would take to cut a hair, and bystanders are unable to tell the exact frame of mind he is in, but it is known to the Buddha and to the dying man himself. Besides, the so-called three desires[10] are at that moment awakened within him, and demons try to take advantage of him, so that he loses his composure of mind. Now one's religious adviser is powerless to remove such affections and it is by the power of the Amida Buddha alone that it can be done. We may depend upon it that the saying is true, 'the cords of all the evil *karma* are powerless to bind' (the one who calls on the sacred name)."

The Buddha's Welcome to Paradise

"A certain man who was praying for the life beyond, once said that if one only keeps his mind composed and says the *Nembutsu*, the Buddha will come to welcome him. But it is said in the *Small Amida Sūtra* that, 'the Buddha with all his retinue is right in front of the dying man, so that when he passes away, he has no distress of mind, but is born into that Land of Perfect Bliss.' Now the point to be observed is that just as one comes to the end of life, the Amida Buddha comes with His holy retinue right before the man's very eyes. It is after he has seen them, that his mind is no longer in distress, and so he attains birth into the Land of Bliss. Instead of praying that when we die it may be of some very light disease, it would be better to spend the same time, when in health, in saying the *Nembutsu* over even once, so that when the end does come you may be favored with the Amida Buddha's welcome, be able to get rid of those three evil desires, and with composed mind be born into the Blissful Land. And yet right here there is need for caution. It does not mean that when you come to die you have no need at all of a religious adviser,

[9] Eight kinds of pain are inherent in human life: 1) birth-pains, 2) pains of age, 3) pains of disease, 4) of death, 5) of parting with loved ones, 6) of meeting with what one dislikes, 7) of not obtaining what one seeks, 8) of the five powerful elements.

[10] These refer to the mentality of a man at death, on whose approach 1) there arises within him a strong love for wife and children and all that he has, 2) he fears lest he should lose his body, and 3) longs to catch a glimpse of the place into which he is destined to be born.

even though he be of small use to you. But as taught by our great teachers, when the end draws near, you should put an image or picture of the Amida Buddha on the west wall of your room, and, facing westward, listen to the exhortation of your religious advisers who tell you to repeat the *Nembutsu*. This I say is the desirable thing."

No Form of Death Incompatible with the *Nembutsu*

"The fact is no one knows beforehand just how he will die. It may be all of a sudden on the highway, it may be in the toilet, it may be that a man is cut down by a long sword or a dagger, that he is burned to death or drowns; for it is impossible for a man to escape the results of his former evil *karma*. And yet no matter what kind of death a man meets, if he daily practices the *Nembutsu*, and has made up his mind he is going to the Land of Bliss, when he actually comes to the end, Amida, Kwannon, and Seishi[11] do come forth to welcome him to that Land, and we ought so to believe. It says in the *Ōjōyōshū* that quite apart from time, place, or other circumstances, if a man begins to pray for *Ōjō* as he comes near to death, there is no method of salvation comparable with the *Nembutsu*, and truly this is so."

Descent of Amida with the Bodhisattvas Kwannon and Seishi

[11] Two of the highest Bodhisattvas, who always attend upon Amida; Kwannon on his left representing mercy, and Seishi on his right representing wisdom.

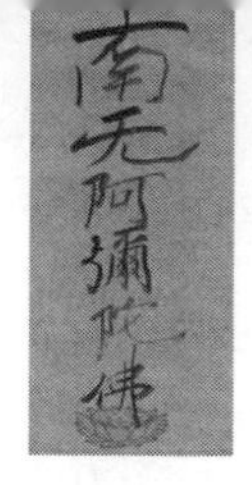

8. A CATECHISM

A man once asked Hōnen some hundred and forty five questions on the heart preparation needed for attaining *Ōjō*, and he answered them all. I now transcribe a few of them.

***Ōjō* Attainable by *Nembutsu* Only**

Question: Is it possible for a man to enter the Pure Land simply by concentration of mind and the repetition of the *Nembutsu*, and doing nothing else, even though his heart undergoes no change?

Answer: It is the rule with common men for their hearts to be in a state of confusion, and it cannot be helped. The only thing is that if men do concentrate their minds upon Amida, and call upon his name, their sin will be destroyed, and they will attain *Ōjō*. Even sins more grievous than that of mental confusion disappear, if men practice the *Nembutsu*.

Fix the Number of Repetitions

Question: Even if we do not fix the number of times for repeating the *Nembutsu* as our daily task, is it not all right to do it as often as one can?

Answer: It is better to fix the number, lest you yield to laziness.

Odors and *Nembutsu*

Question: Ought we to practice the *Nembutsu* after eating leeks, onions, or venison, while the scent of them still remains in the mouth?

Answer: There is nothing whatever in the world that should interfere with the practice of the *Nembutsu*.

Begin with Ten Thousand

Question: How many repetitions of the sacred name should one regard as a day's work?

Answer: Well, the number of *Nembutsu* repetitions may begin with ten thousand, and then go on to twenty, thirty, fifty, sixty, or even a hundred thousand. Everyone should, in his own heart and according to his own will, determine the number within these limits.

Use of the Sacred Cord *Question*: They say that the cord with the five-colored strands is put into the Buddha's left hand, but in which of my hands should it be put, and how drawn (when I come to die)?[1]

Answer: It should be drawn by both hands.

The Merit of Fasting *Question*: Is there any merit in fasting from noon till dawn, and ought one to do it?

Answer: There is merit in such fasting especially on the six days of fasting appointed for each month. But in case there is some matter of great importance, or one is ill, it is not necessary to do it, but only to repeat the *Nembutsu*, and one will thereby get free from the transmigratory round and attain *Ōjō*.

The Merit of Hearing Another's *Nembutsu* *Question*: Even if one does not see a Buddha, or fasten a cord from one's hands to the Buddha's, or even call upon the sacred name oneself, is it possible to be born into the Pure Land at death merely by listening to others repeating the *Nembutsu*?

Answer: It is not always necessary to fasten the cord to one's hand, nor to meet the Buddha face to face, but by means of the *Nembutsu* alone one can attain *Ōjō*. And so long as one has a very deep faith, it is enough to listen to other men's repetitions of the *Nembutsu*.

Can Never Fall from Paradise *Question*: Though one may wish to be eternally free from the experience of birth and death, and never to be born again into this threefold world, is it true, as some say, that, even after one has become a citizen of the Land of Perfect Bliss, the *karma* which has brought him there loses its efficacy, so that he may be born again here into this threefold world?

Answer: Such ideas are entirely wrong. If one is once born into the Land of Bliss, he will never return to this world, but every such one will attain Buddhahood. Only in case one wishes to come back to save others, he may

[1] Amida offers a five-colored cord by which those who have faith in his all-saving grace can be drawn into the Pure Land. A dying believer would be given such a cord to hold; the other end would be attached to Amida's hand in representation of Amida's welcome to the soul.

indeed do so, but by so doing, he does not again return to the round of birth and death. There is nothing better than the practice of the *Nembutsu* to get safely out of this threefold world and be born into the Land of Perfect Bliss. So you ought to practice it most diligently.

Poetry *Question*: Is it a sin to write or recite a poem?

Answer: It is not necessarily wrong. It may indeed become a sin to a man, or it may prove meritorious.

Saké *Question*: Is it a sin to drink *saké*?

Answer: Indeed one ought not to drink, but (you know) it is the way of the world.

Religious Adviser at Death-bed *Question*: When one is about to die, is it enough, in order to attain *Ōjō*, to repeat the *Nembutsu* as one ordinarily does, without calling in a religious adviser?

Answer: Even though no religious adviser comes in, and one is not able to die as painlessly as he desires, he will attain *Ōjō* if only he repeats the *Nembutsu.*

Evil Thoughts *Question*: When evil thoughts keep arising within the mind, what ought one to do?

Answer: The only thing to do is to repeat the *Nembutsu.*

Rinsing the Mouth *Question*: Is it right to call upon the sacred name when going to bed or getting up, without rinsing one's mouth?

Answer: That does not matter.

Leeks and Onions *Question*: How about eating leeks or onions on the six days of the months appointed for fasting?

Answer: It is better not.

The Use of the Rosary *Question*: In one's daily religious exercises, which is the better of the two, telling the beads of the rosary some sixty or a hundred thousand times without stopping to count them one by one, or to do it only some twenty or thirty thousand times, but repeat the *Nembutsu* every time the beads are told?

Answer: It is the usual thing with the ordinary man to find it very hard to act up to the requirements of the Law, even though he sets out to repeat it twenty or thirty thousand times. The point is that you cannot repeat it too often, and so you need to repeat it continuously. It is not that a certain definite number is necessary at all, but that you keep repeating the *Nembutsu*. But we exhort to the repetition of a certain number of times, so that people will not give way to laziness.

Hōnen's radiant rosary

Bodily Purification

Question: After one has eaten fish or fowl, ought he to purify his body before reading the Sūtras?

Answer: The proper way is to read after such purification; not to do so may bring merit, or it may result in sin. Only it is better to read them anyway, even though you do not purify your body.

Reserve Merit

Question: Is it all right to make up on one day for religious duties that were neglected on another day? And may one store up merit now, so as to be forehanded for the future?

Answer: It is all right to make up for past losses. But to be laying up for the future (forgetting the present) would tend to laziness.

Ignorant Priests

Question: Is there any merit in bringing offerings to a lawless or ignorant priest?

Answer: We ought in these latter days to do honor to a lawless and ignorant priest even as to the Buddha.

These words were written by Hōnen's own hand, and inscribed on the back of the *Amida Sūtra*.

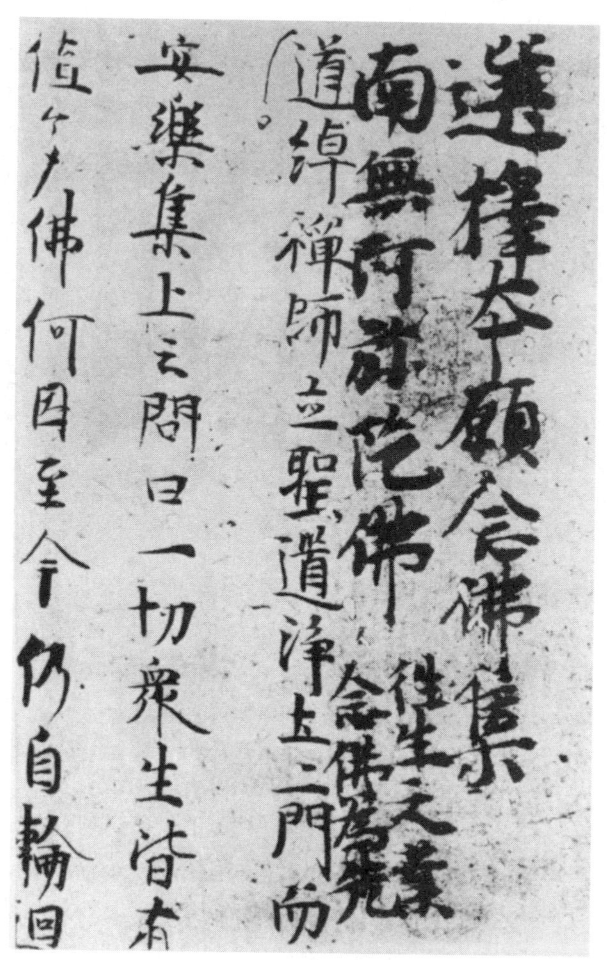

Calligraphy by Hōnen's own hand

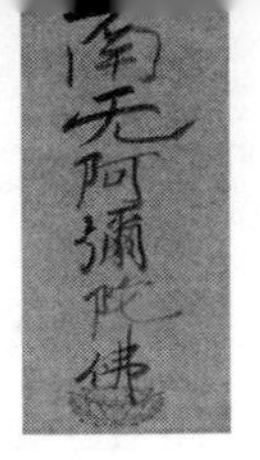

9. HŌNEN ON THE THREE MENTAL STATES

The Meaning of the Three Mental Attitudes

"Anyone who thinks of birth into the Pure Land ought to give attention to what is meant by a religious frame of mind (faith), and also to his outward acts (works), properly adjusting the one to the other. Now in reference to faith, it is stated in the *Meditation Sūtra* that anyone who hopes to be born into that Pure Land must stir himself up to acquire the so-called three attitudes of mind. What three mental attitudes do we mean?

"Well, the first is a most sincere heart, the second is a deep heart, and the third a heart which brings forward one's own merits and pleads them as one condition for the attainment of *Ōjō*. Every one who is possessed of these three mental states will assuredly be born into that land."

A Brief Summary of the Three Mental Attitudes

"The so-called three mental attitudes are nothing else than a deep desire for *Ōjō*. We call that a 'truly sincere heart' which prays without dissimulation or outward display. We call that a 'deep heart' which has not the least particle of doubt of being welcomed into that Land at death, if we but say the *Nembutsu* from our inmost souls. We say a man has 'an earnestly desiring heart' when he desires for himself birth into that Land, and regards all his actions as contributing to the promotion of his *Ōjō*. So he is possessed of these three mental states if he prays without dissimulation, in the conviction that he shall truly attain *Ōjō*."

(a) A "Most Sincere Heart"

"Now what Zendō means by 'the sincere heart' is a heart true to the full, that is, a heart which in every act of the body, in every word of the mouth, and every thought of the mind, is true. In other words, a heart which is not empty within, when pretending great things without, but while loathing this present swiftly passing world, it gives all heed to being completely furnished with that mind which yearns after the way of truth."

(b) A "Deep Believing Heart"

"In the second place, in regard to a deep heart, Zendō says in his *Commentary*, 'A deep heart is one which believes deeply, and may be said to be of two kinds. First of all, we must deeply believe that we are just common mortals possessed of evil passions and sins, and subject to the law of birth and death, and that we have but a small and meager root of goodness within us. Also that we have always from the most remote *kalpas* of past time been subject to transmigration from one state to another, with no relationship to or hope of deliverance therefrom. Then secondly we ought to believe that the Buddha Amida by His Forty-eight Vows[1] can deliver all sentient beings, and that if they call upon His sacred name at least ten times, depending upon His Vow, they shall be certain of birth into the Pure Land, so long as they do not indulge a single thought of doubt. Again a deep heart is one which makes a strong determination to practice the Law according to the teaching of the Buddha, and never to give place to doubt. Do not draw back, nor be moved by any other religious teaching or practice, or any contrary opinion or worldly attachment.'"

(c) Zendō on a "Longing Heart"

"In the third place, regarding what we call a heart which brings its own merits and pleads for their recognition, Zendō has the following exposition: 'By a longing heart Shaka means one which prays for birth into the Pure Land, presenting with a true and deep believing heart (to Amida, in the Land of Bliss), the whole of one's stock of merit, resulting from actions whether worldly or religious performed in the past or present by one's body, mouth, or will, and also that merit which results from regarding with satisfaction similar actions performed by other men, whether common mortals or holy beings. And by the words, a heart which prays for birth into the Pure Land presenting the whole of one's stock of merit, I mean that a man ought to have the thought and conviction of assuredly being born into that land, if he but brings all the merit above-mentioned with a true and sincere heart, deeply believing with a heart as strong as adamant, that is neither moved, confused, nor discomfited, no matter who comes with some opposite teaching or opinion or practice.' Now the meaning of Zendō's exposition is, in the first place, that we must carry in our minds all the merit which we have acquired by action and speech in our former lives, as well as those we are now acquiring, and continue seeking for *Ōjō* right up to the gate of Paradise."

[1] See Glossary under Original Vow.

Sometimes Would Teach, Sometimes Not

Now the fact is that Hōnen sometimes used to teach the need of "the three states of mind," and at others that one does not need to know about them. This depended upon the people to whom he was talking. To a man who believes that by calling upon the sacred name he shall certainly be born into the Pure Land, and who sets his whole heart upon putting his trust in Amida, the three states of mind come naturally of their own accord. But to go to such a man and tell him over and over again, that he ought to have those three mental states will rather only confuse him and hinder his faith. To such a man there is no use at all of insisting upon them. But on the other hand, in the case of a man who is troubled by doubts, and has not yet reached those mental states, if he will but study the holy teachings of the Sūtras, his mind will submit itself to the reasonableness of the doctrine, and he will realize these three states within him. And so it is important for such a man to understand what the nature of those three states is, and it would be wrong for anyone absolutely to deny their importance. If we bear this in mind, we cannot say that there is any inconsistency in Hōnen's holding both views, and urging them on occasion upon others.

The Most Unlettered Are Capable of the "Three Mental States"

"Again in reference to the three mental states, there are some who say that if a man understands them when he repeats the *Nembutsu*, of course he will possess them, but in the case of ignorant people who do not know even the names of those states, how is it possible for them to have them? Now this too, I must repeat, is a great misconception. Even though one is so ignorant as not to know the names of these three mental states, if he only puts implicit trust in Amida's Vow, with no doubt in his heart at all, and thus calls upon the sacred name, he is already in possession of these mental states. And so if one practices the *Nembutsu* with this simple faith, these three mental states arise of their own accord within him. There are, then, even among the most unlettered, those who practice the *Nembutsu*, and when they come to face death, they accomplish their birth into the Pure Land with complete composure of mind. This is a fact of actual experience. There is not the slightest shadow of doubt about it. Whereas on the other hand, there are in fact very many who do a great deal of arguing about these three mental states, about which they know very little, and when they come to die, it is anything but a desirable death. This is something which everyone ought to take seriously to heart."

The *Nembutsu* Includes All Duty

"In my eyes, the meaning of Zendō's commentaries, when he speaks of the three mental states, of the five forms of prayer, and of the four-fold rule for practicing the *Nembutsu*, is that they are all comprehended within the *Namu Amida Butsu*."

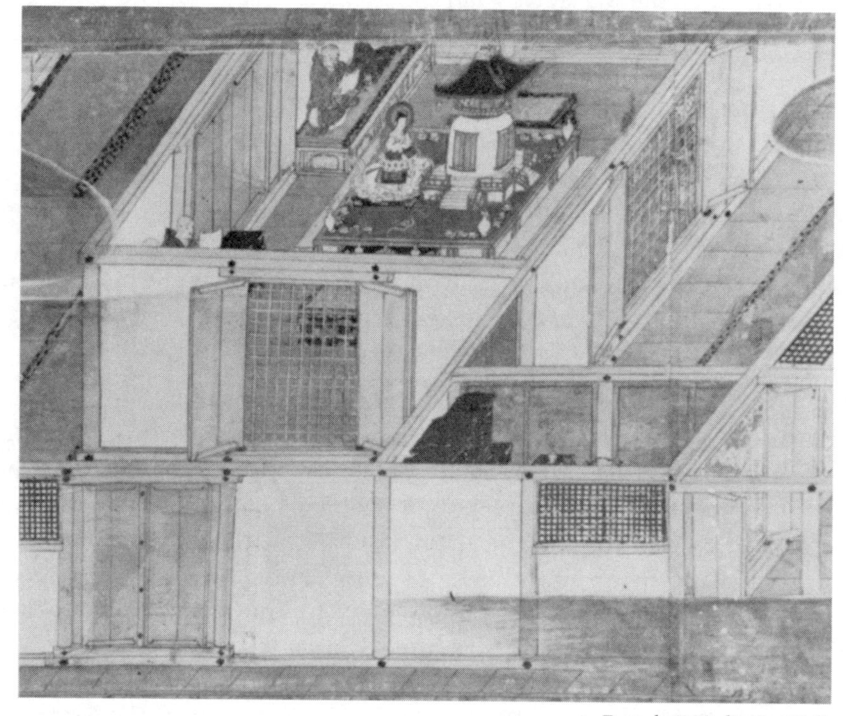

Enryakuji Meditation Hall

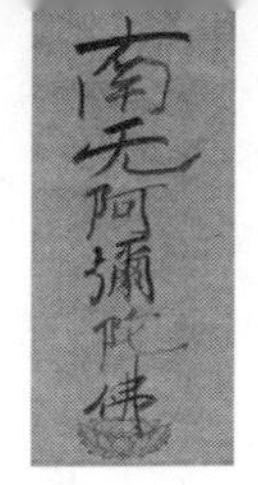

10. GREAT LITERARY WORKS (PART I)

Main Principles of Hōnen's *Senchakushū*

Hōnen's *Senchakushū* was compiled by the order of Kanezane Tsukinowa. I think it is a mirror in which are truly reflected the things essential to securing birth into the Pure Land by means of the *Nembutsu*, and I shall here give a short outline of its main principles.

The title of the first chapter of this book is, "Dōshaku Zenji, the teaching of the Buddha, classified under the two headings, 'Shōdō' and 'Jōdo,' rejecting the former and adopting the latter." In this chapter Hōnen makes a long quotation, which is in the form of a catechism from Dōshaku's work called *Anrakushū* (Chinese: *An-lo-chi*, A Collection of Passages on the Blissful Land), which reads as follows:

(a) The Ordinary Mahāyāna and Hīnayāna Standpoints

"The fact is, no sentient being seriously weighs his own incapacity. If we speak from the ordinary standpoint of the Mahāyāna, there is no one who has really taken to heart what is meant by the 'Truth' 'the Reality' and 'the First Principle of Emptiness.'[1] If again we discuss the Hīnayāna principles, we find that we must, on the one hand, enter first of all into a clear perception of the four truths,[2] and then apply them in actual practice; while on the other hand, we must at the same time shake off the five chains of the lower world of lust,[3] and the five chains of the upper ethereal and spiritual worlds,[4]

[1] Philosophical terms given specific definition by the various sects of the day. Viewed from a practical religious standpoint, these three terms express the same thought as when we say that all sentient beings have the Buddha-nature. That is, even in the midst of human passions with which men struggle, there is in every man that higher nature that the Buddhas possess, which is identical with the absolute reality. Buddhahood therefore is within the reach of all, and is attained when they have transcended the life of illusion.

[2] According to Hīnayāna doctrine, there are four noble truths for us to know and practice: 1) suffering exists, 2) suffering arises from attachment to desires, 3) suffering ceases when attachment to desire ceases, 4) freedom from suffering is possible by practicing the Noble Eightfold Path.

[3] 1) the idea of the reality of our physical body, 2) erroneous conceptions of the precepts, 3) doubts, 4) sexual love, 5) anger.

[4] 1) lust for the ethereal state, 2) lust for consciousness, 3) distraction of mind, 4) pride, 5) ignorance.

Hōnen writing the *Senchakushū*

passing through the four stages leading to the *Arhat*.[5] But whether we ask priest or layman, we find none with the qualifications necessary to put these things into practice. It is only by the practice of the five commandments and the ten good deeds,[6] that one can secure the *karma* which results in birth into the world of humanity, and into the heavenly world. But the truth is that the number able to observe these commandments and good deeds is infinitesimally small. If again we come to consider the fact in connection with the creation of wickedness and sin in the world, it is no whit different from a raging storm of wind and rain. It is for reasons like these that the Buddhas in their great compassion implore men to give themselves up to the Jōdo. Even though men do evil all their lives, if with undivided heart in fervent faith they will but continually call upon the sacred name, they shall be purified from every defilement, and shall surely be born into the Pure Land. How is it that men give no heed to these things, and have no mind for forsaking the evil world?"

[5] To be free from the world of suffering a man must get rid of the world's evil elements, and cultivate good thoughts. To this end he must pass through four stages, known as the four fruits, culminating in becoming an *Arhat*, one who, though in the present world, has already attained *Nirvāna* (literally: "extinction"; liberation from the cycle of rebirth and suffering).

[6] These are the acts which lead to birth in the human and heavenly worlds. The five commandments are: 1) not to kill, 2) not to steal, 3) not to commit adultery, 4) not to lie, 5) not to drink intoxicating liquors. The ten good deeds are: 1) not to kill, 2) not to steal, 3) not to commit adultery, 4) not to lie, 5) not to exaggerate, 6) not to slander, 7) not to be double-tongued, 8) not to covet, 9) not to be angry, 10) not to be heretical.

(b) Hōnen's Counsel to Jōdo Scholars

Then Hōnen says, "I think that scholars of the Jōdo sect ought to note the following. Even though a man has been learning the doctrines of the Shōdō, if his mind turns to the doctrines of the Jōdo, he ought to give up the former and apply himself wholly to the latter. This is the way that Donran did, by giving up his own exposition of the four Śāstras, and devoting himself to the Jōdo. Dōshaku Zenji did the same, abandoning his manifold exertions in the propagation of the *Nirvāna Sūtra*, and giving himself with all diligence to the practice that leads to the Western Paradise.[7] This being the case with men of marked talents in ancient times, how much more should it not characterize us dullards of these later degenerate days!"

(c) The Central Article in Amida's Original Vow

The title of the third chapter is "Passages showing that Amida Nyorai himself made the object of His Original Vow the attainment of birth into the Pure Land by the practice of the *Nembutsu* alone, to the exclusion of all other practices." In this chapter Hōnen quotes from the first volume of the *Larger Sūtra*,[8] and Zendō's *Commentary* thereon, which deal with the Original Vow, and he makes his own explanations in the form of question and answer as follows:

Question: It seems reasonable to reject the bad and choose the good, as mentioned in the articles of the Original Vow. But why is it that Amida rejected all other good deeds, and, in the eighteenth article, chose only the *Nembutsu* as the one by which to attain *Ōjō*?

Answer: It is hard to understand and interpret the holy mind of the Buddha, but I shall try to explain it under two aspects, first, from the standpoint of superiority and inferiority, and secondly from that of ease and difficulty. In regard to the first, the *Nembutsu* is superior and all other practices are inferior, because all virtues are wrapped up in the one sacred name. These, I say, are inherent in the sacred name of the Buddha. For these reasons do we regard the *Nembutsu* as having merits surpassing all others. Not so is it with the other practices, which are all limited to some one aspect. The sacred name is like a house which comprises within it all its constituents,—the beams, rafters, pillars, veranda, and everything else used in the building. But the names of the various parts such as the beams and rafters do not

[7] A term for the Pure Land. See Glossary under Pure Land (Jōdo).

[8] See Glossary under *Larger Sūtra*.

comprise the other parts. We may learn from this the lesson that the merit of calling upon the sacred name surpasses that of all other practices, and that is why I think that Amida rejected the inferior and made the superior His Original Vow.

(d) The **Nembutsu** *the Best and Easiest Way to Salvation*

Hōnen further says, "In the next place, if we look at it from the standpoint of difficulty and ease, the *Nembutsu* is easily practiced, while it is very hard to practice all the other disciplines. For the above reasons thus briefly stated, we may say that the *Nembutsu*, being so easily practiced, is of universal application, while the others being hard to practice, do not suit all cases. And so Amida seemed to have made His Original Vow the rejection of the hard and the choice of the easy way, in order to enable all sentient beings, without distinction, to attain birth into the Pure Land. If the Original Vow required the making of images and the building of pagodas, then the poor and destitute could have no hope of attaining it. But the fact is that the wealthy and noble are few in number, whereas the number of the poor and ignoble is extremely large. If the Original Vow required wisdom and great talents, there would be no hope of that birth for the foolish and ignorant at all; but the wise are few in number, while the foolish are very many. If the Original Vow required the hearing and seeing of a great many things, then people who heard and saw little could have no hope of that birth; but few are they who have heard much, and very many are they who have heard little. If the Original Vow required obedience to the commandments and the Law, then there would be no hope of that birth for those who break the commandments or have not received them; but few are they who keep the commandments and very many are they who break them. The same reasoning applies to all other cases. If, then, we make the Original Vow to consist in the practice of these many forms of discipline, it follows that those who attain birth into Paradise will be few, while the many will fail. We conclude therefore, that Amida Nyorai, when He was a priest by the name of Hōzō ages ago, in His compassion for all sentient beings alike, and in His effort for the salvation of all, did not vow to require the making of images or the building of pagodas conditions for birth into the Pure Land, but only the one act of calling upon His sacred name."

(e) The Conclusion of the Whole Matter

In the last chapter, Hōnen goes on to say, "If then, we wish to get free of the round of birth and death, as there are these two excellent laws, let us, at least for the present, lay aside that of the Shōdō and adopt the Jōdo. And if we would succeed in the Jōdo, which itself has two methods of discipline, the 'miscellaneous' and the 'genuine,'[9] let us reject the former and choose the latter. Again in the 'genuine' too, as there are the so-called 'helpful' practices and the 'essential,' we should give the former the second place in our thought, as an incidental aid, while giving our chief attention to the 'essential.' What we mean by the essential practice is the calling upon the sacred name of the Buddha, which of a certainty issues in birth into the Pure Land, for this is in accord with the Original Vow of the Buddha."

Zendō

[9] Miscellaneous Practices (*zogyo*) are the multitude of practices not related to Amida's Pure Land; Genuine Practices (*shogyo*) are those practices related to Amida's Pure Land. Within the Genuine Practices, the following are "helpful": 1) reading and reciting sūtras, 2) meditation, 3) prostrations, and 4) offerings and praises; the only essential practice, however, is the reciting of the *Nembutsu*.

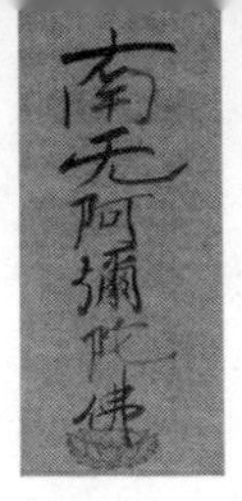

11. GREAT LITERARY WORKS (PART II)

Jōdo in Relation to Buddhism

Hōnen dictated a summary of his doctrines to Seikaku, a priest of *Hōin* (Great Teacher) rank who wrote it out in the following terms:

(a) The Joy of Being Born to Hear the Buddha's Teaching

"In which of the three worlds could I have been wandering, that I failed to meet the revered Shaka in the days of his earthly existence? Which of the four possible births in the rounds of transmigration could have been mine, that I failed to hear Nyorai's preaching of the Law? Alas! I was not among those in attendance on the occasion of his exposition of the Kegon, nor did I hear his sermon on the *Hannya*. I was not present when he was preaching on the summit of the Eagle Mountain about the *Hokke Sūtra*, nor did I manage to get near enough to overhear him expounding the *Nirvāna Sūtra* in the Crane Forest. I must have been staying in one of the houses of those three hundred millions in the land of Śrāvastī, who knew nothing about him. I do not know, but I may have been at the bottom of one of the eight burning hells.[1] Oh! what a shame and pity! Even though one were to be born and reborn countless times through countless *kalpas*, it would be very hard to be born a man, yet I have been so born. And though we were to take myriads of *kalpas* for it, it would be a rare fortune to come in contact with the teaching of the Buddhas. Yet this happiness has come to me. It is indeed a great pity that I did not meet the revered Shaka during his lifetime here, and yet it is surely a reason for rejoicing, that I should have come into the world at a time when the teaching of the Law may be heard everywhere. I am like a blind tortoise in the ocean, that has happily found a home in a floating plank, through which it has at last been able to climb to a place of safety."

(b) The Buddhist View of Human Life

"If we inquire into the history of the spread of Buddhism in our country, we find that it came over here from Korea on the first day of the tenth month in

[1] There are eight burning hells and eight cold ones. On each of the four sides of every burning hell there are four smaller ones, i.e. sixteen around the margins of the eight, making a total of 136. Each hell has its particular torment.

Hōnen conducting a transcription of the *Hokke* ("Lotus") *Sūtra*

the winter of the thirteenth year, i.e. the year of the monkey and water, in the reign of the Emperor Kimmei (540-571). Before that time there had been no propagation of the teaching of the Law, and consequently there was no opportunity to hear about the way of enlightenment. I do not know to what *karma* relation it is due, nor what good deeds we may have done in former existences, but we of the present age are surely to be congratulated on having been born at a time when the Law of the Buddhas prevails everywhere, and we are able to hear about the way of deliverance from that unbearable transmigratory round. All but unattainable though it be, this is happily now our lot. It would then indeed be a most regrettable thing if we were to let our lives be vainly frittered away, without making the most of our rare opportunity. The fact is that we find many idling away their precious time through the long spring days, among the flowers of the Golden Glen. Some pass the long autumn nights gazing at the silver moon from the balconies of their stately southern mansions, while others spend their years racing over the cloud-tipped mountains, hunting deer, or fishing on the ocean wave. Some wend their way through the cold and ice of life's severe winter, while others wipe the hot summer sweat from their brows, as they painfully labor for the gains and sustenance of life. Again we find some powerless to free themselves from those ties of affection for wives and children and loved ones which bind them, while others can never rid themselves of the hatred they feel to those they meet that oppose or ill-treat them.

"The foregoing, then, sums up the life they lead day and night, morning and evening, whether walking, standing, sitting, or lying. They are just living for themselves with all their might, piling up *karma* for the three evil states[2] and eight misfortunes[3] of the future world. It is written somewhere that every act in every moment of the eight hundred million and four thousand moments of every day goes to produce the *karma* of the three evil states. And so each yesterday and today comes and goes, times without number, and all to no purpose. The beautiful flower which opens in the morning is scattered by the evening breeze, while the dew which distils in the evening disappears before the morning sunshine. Thus all ignorant and heedless of these great realities, man still thinks only of earthly glory and immortality. Meanwhile the wind of mutability comes with its ruthless blast, dissolving all created things, and man's mortal body is left bleaching in the wilderness or on some distant mountain, to become at last a moss-covered heap, while the soul wanders alone under solitary skies. Wife, children, and loved ones left lonely in the old home afford him no congenial company, and of no avail are the seven precious stones and ten thousand treasures that fill his storehouses to the brim. All he takes with him are bitter tears of regret. At length, he reaches the assize of Emma the lord of hell, who fixes his degree of guilt, whether small or great, with its proper penalty, light or heavy, addressing him as follows: 'Why should a man like you, born in a land where the Laws of the Buddhas are everywhere known, have come back here after wasting your time, neglecting your religious duties?' What do you suppose you could say to this? Let me beg of you to seek diligently the way of deliverance, that you may not return to the miseries of the three evil states."

(c) Shaka's All-Comprehensive Teaching

"Now we find in the many teachings the great Master himself promulgated during his lifetime, all the principles for which the eight Buddhist sects, the esoteric and exoteric and the Greater and the Lesser Vehicles stand, as well as those elementary doctrines suited to the capacity of the immature, together with those intended for people able to grasp reality itself. Since then there have been various expositions and commentaries on them such as we

[2] 1) hell, 2) the realm of hungry ghosts, 3) animality, which can be interpreted also as states of mind. See Glossary under Three Evil States.

[3] This refers to the eight unfortunate places or states, so called because those who are born there are not able to see a Buddha, or hear his sermons. The first three are the so-called "three evil states," then 4) the heaven of long life, 5) the northern continent, 6) deformity, 7) sophism or paganism, 8) a period without a Buddha.

now have, with their multitude of diverse interpretations. Some expound the principle of the utter emptiness of all things. Some bring us to the very heart of reality, while others set up the theory that there are five fundamental distinctions in the natures of sentient beings, and still others reason that the Buddha-nature is found in them all. Every one of these sects claims that it has reached finality in its world view, and so they keep contending with one another, each persisting in saying that its own is the most profound and is absolutely right. Now the fact is that what they all say is exactly what the Sūtras and Śāstras say, and corresponds with the golden words of Nyorai himself, who, according to men's varying capacity, taught them at one time one thing and at another time another, as circumstances required. So it is hard now to say which is profound and which is shallow, or to distinguish their comparative value, for they are all equally taught, and we must not go to either extreme in our interpretation. If we but attend to our religious practices as the Sūtras teach, they will all help us to pass safely over the sea of birth and death to the other shore. If we act according to the Law, we shall attain enlightenment. Those who go on vainly disputing as to whether a color has a light or dark shade, are like deaf men talking about the quality of a man's voice whether it is good or bad. The one thing to do is to put the principles into practice, because they all teach the way of deliverance from the dread bondage."

(d) The Holy Path and Pure Land Ways of Salvation

"Dōshaku was the first priest to differentiate the Buddhist sects by classifying them under the two general divisions of Holy Path (*Shōdō*) and Pure Land (*Jōdo*). By the Holy Path is meant the way a man even in this corrupt world can get free from his evil passions, and attain enlightenment, while by the gate of the Pure Land is meant the way to secure this by being born into the Land of Bliss at death. Now in reference to the Pure Land method of salvation, as laid down in the *Meditation Sūtra*, it must be said that there is not only one single condition required, but many; for it speaks of the so-called three good deeds leading to blessedness, the discipline necessary, and the thirteen kinds of meditation. By the thirteen meditations are meant meditation first on the sun, second on the water, third on the land, fourth on the treasure trees, fifth on the treasure lakes, sixth on the treasure halls, seventh on the lotus stands, eighth on the images of the Buddha and Bodhisattvas occupying them, ninth on the real body of Amida Buddha, tenth on that of Kwannon, eleventh on that of Seishi, twelfth on all the stages of his own development, and thirteenth on all the foregoing considered severally or together.

"Then the three good deeds leading to happiness are all practicable by men in the non-meditative stage. They are each divided into three as follows: First, those having to do with so-called worldly goodness, namely, 1) filial devotion to and the support of one's parents, and the service of one's teachers and elders; 2) killing no living being, but treating them with kindness; 3) the practice of the tenfold goodness. Second, those having to do with moral goodness, namely, 1) devotion to the Three Treasures, i.e. the Buddhas, the Law, and the Church; 2) the perfect observance of all the precepts; 3) no violation of any of the rules of propriety. Third, those having to do with religious goodness, namely, 1) the desire for enlightenment; 2) deep belief in the law of moral causation; 3) reading and reciting the Mahāyāna Sūtras, and persuading others to practice the teachings of the same. This is stated in detail in the *Meditation Sūtra*.

"To sum up what we have said, no discipline necessary for the attainment of *Ōjō* is omitted from the foregoing category of meditative and non-meditative goodness. So let a man decide upon which of these is most congenial to his own nature, and apply himself with all diligence to that, up to the measure of his own capacity, and he will find that each and every one will bring him to birth into the Pure Land. Let him be in no doubt whatever about this."

(e) Jōdo Better Suited to Our Capacities

"But if we inquire into the essential nature of these various disciplines, we find that the number of the meditative reaches thirteen, and of the non-meditative nine, and they are all difficult to practice. Anyone who would enter the gate of the meditative will find that his mind races about like a horse among the six objects of sensation, and when he wants to get near to the gate of the non-meditative, he is like a monkey that sports on the branches of the tree of the ten evils. Try as he will to quiet his mind and subdue his heart, he finds himself unable to do so. If, however, we now examine the last three of the practices, we find it explained in the Sūtra, that even when a man addicted to the ten evils, or one guilty of the five deadly sins, draws near to death, if he should meet a teacher who will tell him to call upon the sacred name of Amida, ten times or even once, he will be born into the Pure Land. Here we surely have something just suited to our several capacities, have we not?"

(f) Never Revile the Buddhas' Laws, the **Nembutsu** *One*

"Now there are some scholars who are opposing the *Nembutsu*, on the ground that its general practice would result in the decline of the other Buddhist sects, and it would appear as if a large number of people, on this account, have been giving it up. This is surely a most regrettable state of affairs. Buddhism is a system destined to continue for ten thousand years; and no matter if some should like to do away with it, this is beyond human power, because Buddhism is under the benign protection of the many *devas* and good divinities.[4] We have an example in the history of our own country of an attempt on the part of Moriya to destroy Buddhism utterly and drive it from the country; but its life is not gone yet, as you can plainly see, for it still goes on spreading down to our own times. How much less possible then, it must surely be, for the ignorant, whether priests or laymen, men or women, to ruin the Hossō, Sanron, Tendai, or Kegon sects by practicing the *Nembutsu*. If men were to give it up, do you think that would promote the prosperity of any of the other sects? Would it enable them to fathom the mysteries of the many sects any better, if they lightly abandoned the practice of the *Nembutsu*? Would it not rather be a great loss all round? Do you suppose that the distinguished scholars of the head temples in the southern and northern capitals, who inherit the traditions of all the exoteric sects, and of the esoteric also, with their twofold doctrine of reason and practical wisdom, would have nothing more to do with their own sects, simply because the *Nembutsu* cult has spread abroad over the country a hundred, a thousand, or even ten-thousand fold?"

(g) **Ōjō** *Is for All Alike*

"Those who think that it is only the *Nembutsu* of the pious and learned which can eventuate in *Ōjō*, and that there is no *Ōjō* for the ignorant and unlettered, and those who go on sinning every day, even if they should say the *Nembutsu*, have not yet grasped the fact that the Original Vow includes both the good and the bad. Those who fail to understand the meaning of this truth will doubt their own powers, and not obtain *Ōjō*. It is impossible in this life to change man's nature, which he has inherited through the working of his *karma* from a preexistent state. Those who call upon the sacred name should do it with the nature they now have, the wise man as a wise man, the fool as a fool, the pious as pious, the irreligious as irreligious, and

[4] The Japanese Buddhist idea in regard to the Brahmanistic deities of India or the Shintō deities of Japan is that they are real existences, and that they have become the protectors of Buddhism.

thus all equally may attain *Ōjō*. Whether a man is rich and noble, or poor and mean, whether he is kind or unkind, avaricious or morose, indeed no matter what he is, if he only repeats the *Nembutsu*, in dependence upon the mysterious power of the Original Vow, his *Ōjō* is certain. Amida's Original Vow was made to take in all conceivable cases of people, whom He thus engaged to save, if they would but practice the *Nembutsu*. Without inquiring at all into the grade of their several capacities, but merely saying the *Nembutsu* in their simple earnestness—this is all that is needed for anybody. Bear in mind that everyone who thinks the *Nembutsu Ōjō* is too lofty or too profound to be grasped has wholly misapprehended the very nature of the Original Vow itself. We say that the sinner who is powerless in himself to do anything can find his way to that Blissful Land, by dependence upon that Original Vow and the *Nembutsu* repetitions. Now this is the same as dependence upon the Vow of the 'Other-Power,' or what is sometimes called 'the world-transcending Vow.'"

(h) The Superiority of the Jōdo

"When we say that the Jōdo is superior to all other sects, and that the *Nembutsu* is superior to all other religious disciplines, we mean that it provides salvation for all classes of sentient beings. Of course meditation upon the Absolute, heart longing for perfect knowledge (*bodhi*), the reading and reciting of the Mahāyāna Sūtras, the mystic practices of the Shingon, the meditation of the Tendai, and so on, all belong to the Law of the Buddhas, reveal their superiority, and tell us how to cross over the sea of birth and death. And yet on the other hand, they are quite beyond the capacity of

Enshrining of the transcribed *Hokke Sūtra*

people living in these latter degenerate times. After the ten thousand years of these latter evil days have passed, the average length of human life is to be shortened to ten years, and many will degenerate so that they will be guilty of the ten evil deeds and the five deadly sins, and yet the whole of them, old and young, male and female, all without exception, are included within the scope of that Original Vow, and are given the assurance that they will be cared for and never forsaken, if they will but repeat the *Nembutsu* ten times, or even once. This is why we insist that the *Nembutsu* quite outrivals all the other sects and disciplines."

(i) Nembutsu *and Daily Living*

"If we only put our trust in Amida's Original Vow, there is no doubt whatever about our future destiny, but what are we to do with the present world? Well, the thing to do is to make the *Nembutsu* practice the chief thing in life, and to lay aside everything that you think may interfere with it. If you cannot stay in one spot and do it, then do it when you are walking. If you cannot do it as a priest, then do it as a layman. If you cannot do it alone, then do it in company with others. If you cannot do it and at the same time provide yourself with food and clothing, then accept the help of others and go on doing it. Or if you cannot get others to help you, then look after yourself but keep on doing it. Your wife and children and domestics are for this very purpose, of helping you to practice it, and if they prove an obstacle, you ought not to have any. Friends and property are good, if they too prove helpful, but if they prove a hindrance they should be given up. In short, there is nothing that may not help us to *Ōjō*, so long as it helps us to go on the even tenor of our way through life undisturbed. Men take the very best care of their bodies, and refuse to cast them off, even though they know they are destined to return to the three worlds of evil. How tenderly should we care for our bodies, and how earnestly should we practice the *Nembutsu*, when we know that our destiny is birth into the Pure Land. Any one whose one object of desire is such a care of his body as to minister only to the enjoyment of the present life, and not rather to help him in his *Nembutsu* practice, is doing what belongs to the three evil states. Whereas, if one's object of desire is such a care of himself as promotes his blissful *Ōjō*, he will find that that desire contributes to that end."

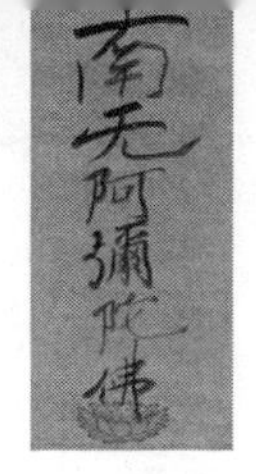

12. HŌNEN'S POEMS

Hōnen was not in the habit of writing poetry, but, following the customs of his country, he wrote a few poems bearing upon the doctrines of his sect, which, in condensed form give expression to his inner thoughts. Some of these have been handed down to us by his disciples, while others were published after his death, as poems written by his own hand.

Spring

O mist of spring, thou hidest all things beautiful and bright,
As if there did not shine the true, imperishable light!

Summer

I gaze and gaze each passing day
On the geranium[1] sweet,
And for the happy day I yearn
My Amida to meet.

Autumn

If from Buddha Amida
My heart its col'ring gains,
It will be like the beauteous boughs
In autumn's crimson stains.

[1] There is an interesting play on the word here. The first syllable in the Japanese word for geranium suggests the sound of the word for "meeting," so that whenever he looked upon a geranium he thought of "meeting" the Buddha.

Winter

If in the winter of our sin,
Amida's name we call,
Warm rays from Him will chase away
The cold and snowdrifts all.

Sacrifice

Composed to bring out the idea that when a man comes in contact with the teachings of the Buddha he must be prepared, if necessary, to sacrifice even his life to obtain its benefits:

Dear life itself is not too dear
For woman's love to give.
For joys eternal, then, why fear
To sacrifice and live?

My Mountain Home

Composed in the Kachiodera Temple:

Above the thatch of my mountain home
The white clouds morning and evening hover.
Ah! When shall the hour of that day come
That the *Ōjō* purple me shall cover?[2]

Exclusive Practice

Composed to show that in order to attain birth into the Land of Perfect Bliss, a man should give up all other forms of discipline, and devote himself solely to the practice of the Nembutsu *prescribed in Amida's Original Vow.*

[2] In reference to the purple clouds that hover over the place where a man is just about to attain *Ōjō*.

Ill seems each occupation
That would free the heart from blame,
Compared with invocation
Of the Buddha's sacred name.

Seek the Land of Bliss in Youth

To seek the Land of Bliss
In early years
Will leave for life's fair end
No doubts or fears.

The Cicada

Like the cicada that has cast
Its shell but sings its rapturous lay,
The voice of him who call His name
From the frail body of this clay,
His heart to scenes of Paradise
Already having flown away.

Amida's Light

The Sūtra says: "Amida's light illumines all sentient beings throughout the ten worlds, who call upon the sacred name, protects and never forsakes them."

There is no place where the moonlight
Casts not its cheering ray;
With him who has the seeing eye
Alone that light will stay.

The "Most Sincere Heart"

In quest of *Ōjō*, need it be that any fall?
Sincerity of heart is lacking, that is all.

Nembutsu

To be repeated ten times just as you go to sleep:

Ten times Amida's name shall pass my lips
Ere I repose.
My last long slumber shall begin some time,
And when,—who knows?

The following poems were written by Hōnen's own hand:

The Pine of a Thousand Years

Pine of a thousand earthly years,
I dwell beneath thy shade,
Till by the Lord of Boundless Life
My welcome home is made.

The Little Pine

'Tis called the little pine,—I marvel why,
Its towering branches seem to touch the sky.

The Heart of Man

The heart of man is like the water of a mere:
You know not whether it will be turbid or clear.

The Precious Memory of Old Friends

First in the Blessed Pure Land
When I attain my birth
Shall be the precious memory
Of friends I left on earth.

The Glorious Vision of the Pure Land

The Pure Land's glorious vision
Is bliss that man may claim,
If he but worthily repeats
Amida's sacred name.

The eighth day of the twelfth month of the second year of Genkyū (1205). (Signed) Genkū.

Garden at Katsura

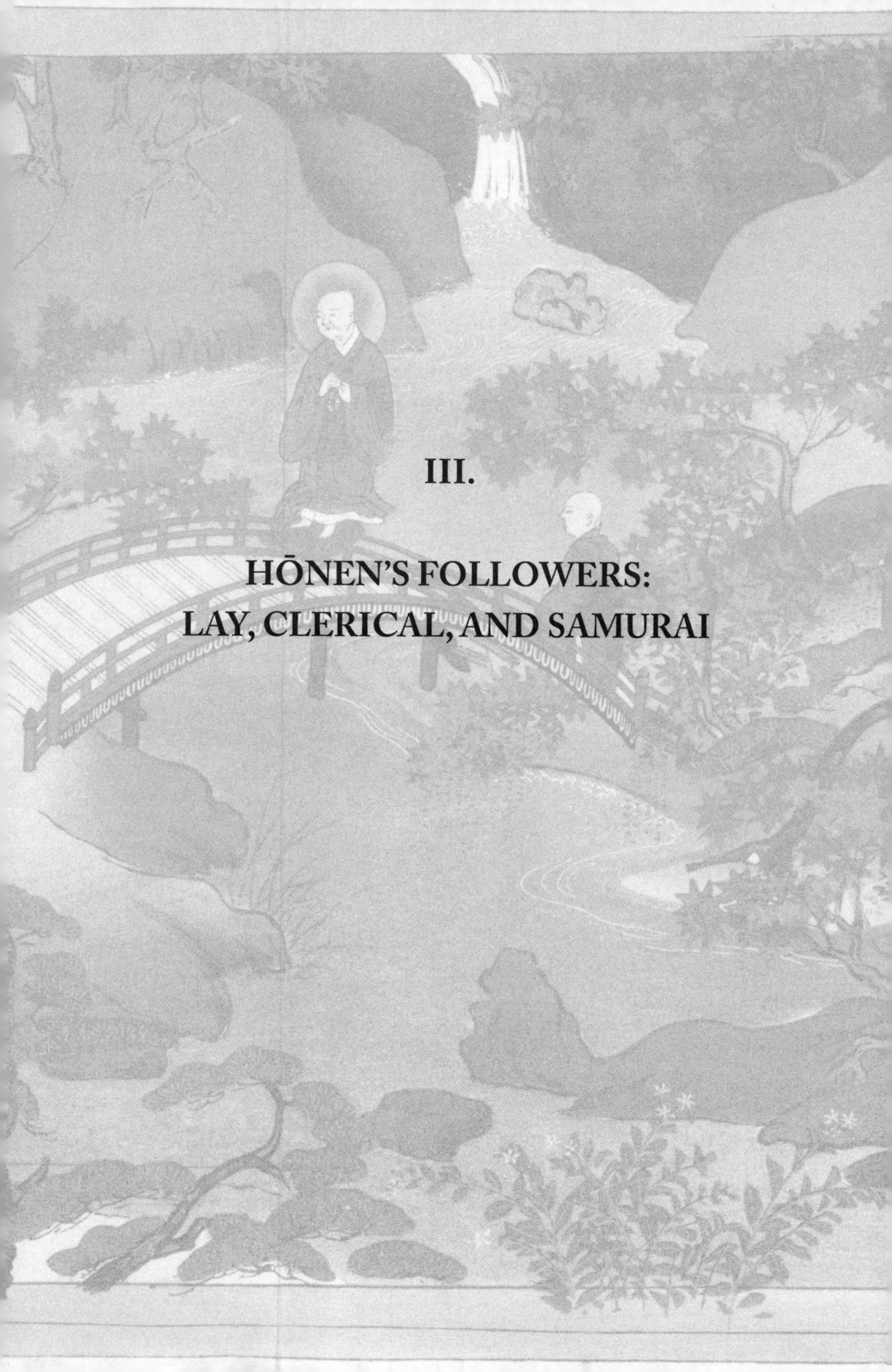

III.

HŌNEN'S FOLLOWERS: LAY, CLERICAL, AND SAMURAI

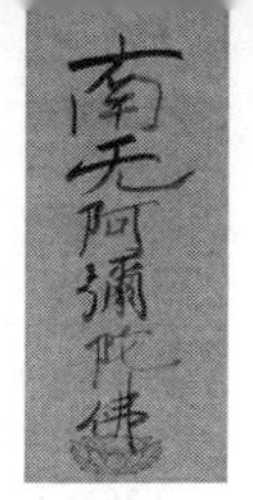

13. THE IMPERIAL CONFIDENCE IN HŌNEN

The Emperor Takakura Taking the Vows

In the spring of the fifth year of the reign of Jōan (1175), in the reign of the Emperor Takakura, Hōnen, on the invitation of His Majesty, visited the palace to administer to him the sacrament of the perfect precepts of the One Vehicle. It was at this time also that the Court officials and ladies of high rank took upon themselves the same vows. During the period of Jōkwan (859), in the reign of the Emperor Seiwa, Jikaku Daishi was invited to the Imperial palace called Shishiiden, and both the Emperor and Empress at that time pledged their devotion to the perfect precepts. So Hōnen, as Jikaku's ninth successor, endowed as he was with the full powers of his master, hereby revived this ancient ceremony in the Imperial family—surely a most meritorious deed.

The Emperor Go-Shirakawa's Regard for Hōnen

The retired Emperor Go-Shirakawa invited Hōnen to the Hōjūji palace to administer the sacrament by which he again took upon himself the vow of obedience to the perfect precepts. On this occasion, the Emperor summoned some of the learned scholars of the Sammon and Onjō Temples, and had them lecture in turn from their several standpoints on the *Ōjōyōshū*, when Hōnen also opened the book and delivered a lecture, in which he emphasized the passage which says that the teaching and practice of the principles essential for birth into the Pure Land of Bliss are like eyes and feet to people in these latter degenerate days, and so both high and low, priests and people, should take refuge therein. As the Emperor listened, it was as if the truth had seized him for the first time, and he was moved to tears. So profound was his regard for Hōnen, that he ordered Takanobu, the Vice-Mayor of the right section of the capital to paint a portrait of the holy man, and deposit it in the treasure-house of the Rengeōin Temple in Kyōto—an incident almost unprecedented in our history.

Hōnen Declines Official Appointment

An instruction was issued by the Emperor Go-Shirakawa appointing Hōnen Chief official Commissioner for the raising of funds required for the reconstruction of the

Tōdaiji Temple, and His Excellency Yukitaka, Chief Secretary of the Supreme Council, was sent to Hōnen to ask him to accept the appointment. Hōnen flatly declined the honor, saying, "I left the community at Sammon (Mount Hiei), and retired to a quiet place among the trees and streams, where I might in solitude give myself to the observance of the laws of the Buddhas, and particularly of the *Nembutsu*. If now I were to accept such a position as this, I should have to be occupied in all sorts of most exacting official duties, which would seriously interfere with the one purpose of my life." Yukitaka, seeing that Hōnen was firm in his determination, told the Emperor, and he ordered that if a man of faculty could be found among Hōnen's disciples, one should be chosen. Whereupon Shunjōbō Chōgen of Daigo was appointed, and went at once to the great shrine of the Sun Goddess[1] in the province of Ise, to pray for some good omen to be given as an assurance that he could complete the work. He went on praying night and day for three weeks, and at dawn on the twenty first day, as, from sheer weariness, he fell into a slight doze. He had a dream in which he saw a lady dressed in Chinese garments presenting him with a precious gem, an inch square in size. On waking, there the gem was right on his sleeve. At the sight of it, Chōgen was in raptures, and stowed it carefully away. After this, when the announcement of the rebuilding was issued, there was an immediate response on the part of the public, and all the funds required were subscribed, so that in but a short time a bronze image of the Buddha was cast, and came out as beautiful as the one that had been destroyed.

The Emperor Go-Shirakawa's Happy Death

The Emperor Go-Shirakawa was thus deeply impressed by Hōnen's teaching, and developed a faith quite out of the ordinary, accumulating much merit by repeating the sacred name a million times. This he did two hundred times over—a thing indeed without parallel. He began to be indisposed on the fifth day of the fifth month in the third year of Kenkyū (1192), and as he daily grew worse, he sent for Hōnen to come and act as his religious counselor. Hōnen accordingly on the twenty sixth day of the second month repaired to the palace, and gave him the sacrament of the perfect precepts, prescribing the ceremony appointed for the dying,[2] as a preparation for his birth into the Pure Land. Of course he had given daily attention to these things all along,

[1] In Japanese, Amaterasu, one of the most important native Shinto deities.

[2] This ceremony consists of various pious exercises. A picture of Amida accompanied by twenty five Bodhisattvas coming down from the Land of Bliss to welcome the person about

but Hōnen kindly and gently reminded him of these truths, to the deepening of his faith, so that he did not weary of repeating the sacred name. On the twelfth day of the third month at the hour of the dog (8 p.m.), they brought in an image of Amida, and on the thirteenth at the hour of the tiger (4 a.m.), facing death with calm and undisturbed mind, he breathed his last, in the act of repeating the *Nembutsu*. He passed away in a sitting posture just like one who falls asleep, and thus finally attained his long cherished desire of birth into the Pure Land. He was sixty six years of age at the time. It seems evident that his happy death must have been due to his relations with Hōnen in a former state of existence.

Tablet of the *Nembutsu*

to die, is placed within sight of the invalid, as also a standing image of Buddha, on whose left hand a five-colored cord is fastened, with the other end of the cord in the right hand of the patient. Relatives and friends gathered in the room sing a hymn expressing the desire of all that Amida will come to welcome his followers to his Land of Bliss. A religious adviser takes his seat near the bed. A bell is rung in order to shut out all other sounds and help the invalid to concentrate his mind upon the one object of desire. This is frequently repeated if it is supposed that death is drawing near.

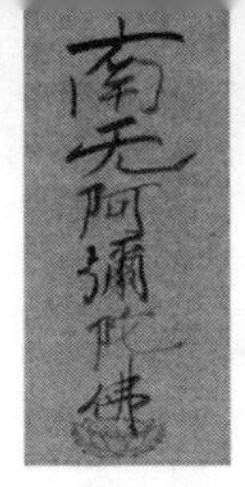

14. HŌNEN'S CLERICAL FOLLOWERS

Prince Jōe's Conversion and Happy Death

Jōe, a Prince of the Blood who bore the *Shinnō* title,[1] was the abbot of the Shōgoin Temple. He was taken dangerously ill. All the resources of medical science were exhausted upon him, but to no purpose. Then Bishops Gyōshun and Kōin, together with a number of other priests of the Onjōji Temple, held a meeting to pray for his recovery, when they united in the reading of the *Daihannya Sūtra*. The rank of these priests among their associates would be similar to that of the argus pheasant and phoenix among birds, or the dragon and elephant among animals. But in spite of all, the patient was becoming worse and worse. Expecting no further help from these priests, they sent for Hōnen, who, although asked twice, did not respond to their invitation but declined to go. Thereupon for the third time they sent a messenger to him, this time Jisshō Risshi, who urged him by all means to come and instruct the sick man in the principles of the *Nembutsu*. He urged so earnestly that at last Hōnen, thinking the Prince was destined to be born into the Pure Land, hurried along with the Risshi in his carriage to the sick chamber. As soon as he met the Prince, the latter said to him, "How may one escape from the world of birth and death? Pray help me into the way of future blessedness." Hōnen at once explained to him what one ought to do at the time of one's death, and then went on to the Original Vow of Amida Buddha. As he proceeded, tears of joy flowed down the cheeks of the sick man, and, with his face towards Hōnen, he folded his hands in profound reverence. Afterwards Hōnen returned home, and the next day the Prince passed away to the Pure Land. Towards the end he repeated the *Nembutsu* fifteen thousand times. Indeed he stopped breathing in the act of repeating the sacred name. All who were in attendance were filled with joy at his happy death, and were high in their praises of the virtue of Hōnen. When Jisshō afterwards told Hōnen of the manner of the Prince's death, he too rejoiced.

Jōgon's Doubts Dispelled

Hōin Jōgon, the chief priest of the Chikurimbō Temple, situated in the eastern part of the compound of the great

[1] A title given to princes who were the sons and brothers of the Emperor.

Enryakuji Temple, once visited Hōnen in his place of retirement at Yoshimizu, and asked him how in this present life we may escape from the round of birth and death. Hōnen replied, "That is the very question which I, Genkū, wish to ask you." To which Jōgon answered, "It may be that on the speculative side of the question you have still some problems unsolved, but on the practical side, as to how we may free ourselves from the bondage of the world, as you are a man of large attainments in knowledge and virtue, and of profound faith and religious experience, I think you must already have come to some satisfactory conclusion."

To this Hōnen said, "I know of no other way of reaching the supreme bliss of birth into the Pure Land than by taking advantage of Amida's Original Vow." The Hōin replied, "I too think the same, but I asked you in order to confirm my own conviction by your superior wisdom. Although what you say is true, what ought one to do when evil thoughts and passions come surging through his mind?" Hōnen then said, "This is the working of the natural evil disposition of man, and the ordinary man is powerless to control it. But I am sure that deliverance and birth into the Pure Land may be obtained by wholly relying upon the Original Vow of Amida, by calling upon the sacred name, and taking advantage of the power of the Buddha's Vow." On hearing this, Jōgon's doubts were immediately dissolved, and he was able with all his heart to exercise a firm and unshaken faith, and withdrew with the remark that he had not a single doubt left on the subject.

Hōnen's Instruction to the Vicar-General

When Hōnen was staying at the Tennōji Temple, Myōhen, the Vicar-General, paid a visit to the Zenkōji Temple, and on his way called on Hōnen, who, when he heard from his servant of the Vicar-General's arrival, came out into the reception room and invited him in. No sooner had Myōhen taken his seat, than he asked Hōnen how one may in this life get free from the painful transmigratory round. To this Hōnen at once replied, "In order to accomplish one's birth into the Pure Land, there is no way comparable to that of calling upon Amida's sacred name." Whereupon the Vicar-General said, "Yes, of course everyone recognizes this; but when we are calling upon the Buddha, what are we to do when our minds are all in confusion, and evil thoughts arise within us?" Hōnen said in reply, "Who indeed, born into this troubled world of desire, can keep his mind free from its distractions? How can the common man, burdened with inward passion and illusion, shake himself free from impure thoughts? I, Genkū, myself am powerless to suppress the like. When one's mind is thus distracted, and such evil thoughts

come rushing in, if one takes the sacred name into his lips, he will by virtue of the Original Vow of Amida certainly be born into the Pure Land." "It was just to hear this that I came to see you," said the Vicar-General, and presently he withdrew. The people noticing that this was the first time for him to meet Hōnen, he retired from his presence without a single word of the ordinary formalities of intercourse, and they could not help admiring him. As Hōnen went back into his room, he remarked, "How hard it is to silence the mind, to prevent evil thoughts from arising, and to put one's whole soul into the calling upon the sacred name. It is like taking out one's eyes or cutting off one's nose."

Hōnen on the Awakening of Faith

Hōnen once said, "There used to be a priest of the Tendai sect, who was very diligent in the study of the Jōdo doctrines. With a sigh he once remarked, 'I have already come to understand the main points in this teaching, and yet somehow a believing heart has not yet been stirred within me. What can I do to awaken such faith?' I gave him the following injunction: 'Pray to the Three Treasures.' After a long time he came to me and said, 'I have been in the habit of offering prayers according to your instructions, and I happened one day to be repairing to the Tōdaiji Temple. It was the very day on which the ridge-poles of the new building were to be raised, and in some strange way that I could hardly comprehend, these immense timbers were lifted up through the air by windlasses, as easily and quickly as if they had been flying. As I stood gazing at it, to my surprise they were put down just in the

Myōhen dreams of Hōnen

right spot. "Such indeed," thought I, "is the skill of a carpenter in his work. How much more perfect and skilful then must be the art of Amida Nyorai in saving men." And as I thought of it, my doubts all disappeared in a trice, and a settled faith laid hold of me. But, as I think of it, this was nothing but the result of my daily prayer to the Three Treasures.' I suppose, it was some three years after this, that, amid happy omens, he accomplished his desire for birth into the Pure Land. It must be remembered that the receiving of instruction and the awakening of faith are in their nature quite distinct from each other. In his case, he did not reach the experience of faith while studying the doctrines, but it was awakened within him by merely looking at this external phenomenon. And so I say that in the great majority of cases, even though a man hears the Jōdo doctrines, and begins the *Nembutsu* practice, if faith does not spring up within him, be should apply his mind diligently, always keep thinking the matter over and over, and also keep praying to the Three Treasures."

Hōnen's Dedication of the Temple Built by Munesada

A subordinate official (*Sakwan*) in the Left Gate Guards' office of the Imperial palace, Munesada Fujiwara, and his wife, were of one mind in their desire to build a temple. So they chose a lot for the purpose on the northeastern side of the Ungoji Temple, and the framework of the building was raised on the ninth day of the fourth month of the first year of Kennin (1201), the structure being completed in the following spring. The principal image placed in the temple was that of Amida, with those of

Kwannon and Jizō[2] beside it. In the autumn of this same year, Hōnen went from his residence at Yoshimizu to the Shōō Mida-in, one of the temples belonging to the Ungoji, to stay for a hundred days. Here he found Munesada, the promoter of the building enterprise, kneeling in front of the gate. After explaining to him the reason for his building the temple, he asked Hōnen to conduct the dedication ceremony. In compliance therewith, Hōnen entered the temple, and observed the way in which the idols had been enshrined. Forthwith he went out of the temple saying, "This is no temple for me to dedicate." Munesada could not understand what Hōnen meant, and was greatly embarrassed, when someone told him that "everyone says that Hōnen is an incarnation of Seishi, but you have no image of Seishi in your temple.[3]

The Bodhisattva Seishi

[2] Jizō (Sanskrit: Kshitigarbha), a popular Bodhisattva known to alleviate suffering, particularly of those already condemned to hell.

[3] One of the highest Bodhisattvas, who always attend upon Amida; Kwannon on his left representing mercy, and Seishi on his right representing wisdom. Seishi Maru is also the birth name of Hōnen.

Probably that is what displeases him." At this Munesada hastened to have an image of Seishi made, and, after removing that of Jizō to another part of the temple, he set up Seishi's image in its place. Availing himself of another opportunity when Hōnen was visiting the Ungoji Temple, on the last day of the eighth month of the second year of Kennin (1202), he asked him again to conduct the dedication ceremony, when Hōnen at once consented, but, instead of using the opening sentences of the ordinary ritual prescribed, he only repeated the sacred name a thousand times. Then he had the continuous repetition of the sacred name commenced here, and gave to the temple the name of Injōji. It is still standing, with the image of the Bodhisattva Jizō behind that of Seishi.

The Bodhisattva Kwannon

15. HŌNEN'S FOLLOWERS—LAY AND CLERICAL

Hōnen's Letter to the Dying Nun Shōnyobō

A nun by the name of Shōnyobō became deeply attached to the teaching of Hōnen, and earnestly practiced the *Nembutsu*. She was taken sick, and sent word to Hōnen that as she was nearing the end, she would very much like to see him once more. When this word reached him, it happened that he was just then engaged in the so-called special *Nembutsu* practice, so he sent his answer by letter, going into much detail. It ran as follows: "I am very sorry indeed to hear of Shōnyobō's illness. Having heard that she is ill, in fact seriously so, I should like to go and see her, and make sure whether she is going right on with the practice of the *Nembutsu* up to the very end; but especially so, when I remember how often she used to call upon me to ask questions about the way of salvation. So as soon as word reached me, I at once wanted to go and see her. But I had just before that decided upon the special *Nembutsu* practice for some days, and not to go out of my chamber for anything whatsoever."

(a) Why He Could Not Visit Her

"Now circumstances have so changed, that I am tempted to reverse my decision and go at once to see her. But on further reflection I have come to feel that, after all, it does not matter one way or the other about such interchanges of courtesy in this world, for the fact is that we are in danger anyway of becoming foolishly attached to these earthly bodies of ours. No matter who it is, no one stays forever here in this fleshly body. The only difference is that either I myself or someone else must be left behind and the other go first. Then if we think of the interval of time that will separate us, that too is uncertain. And even though they may call it long, at the longest it is only like a short dream or vision."

(b) The Hope of Meeting Again in the Hereafter

"So no matter how many times I think it over, the more I am convinced that the thing to do is to think only of our meeting in the land of Amida Buddha, where, as we sit upon our lotus flowers, the cares of this world will have all cleared away, and we shall converse together about the scenes and events of our past lives. We shall then take counsel together as to how we may help each other in promoting the salvation of men down through the long future. This is the same as I have always told her from the beginning, that she should take firm hold upon the Buddha's Original Vow, not allowing one thought of doubt to enter her heart. And even though she can only repeat the *Nembutsu* but once, to remember that, however sinful she feels herself to be, she shall, by the power of the Buddha's Vow, without question be born into the Pure Land. So tell her to apply herself with undivided mind to the repetition of the sacred name."

(c) Dependence upon the Buddha's Power the One and Only Condition of Ōjō

"Our birth into the Pure Land is not in the least related to our goodness, or badness, but solely depends upon the Buddha's power. It matters not how high one's rank may be, in these latter evil days, birth into the Pure Land by one's own power is extremely difficult. As it is all by the Buddha's power, however sinful, foolish, or unclean we may be, everything hangs solely upon our trusting in the power of his Original Vow. There are indeed, I am very sorry to say, those who persist in saying that it is quite impossible to attain birth into the Pure Land. But however learned or noble in rank such persons may be, tell her not to pay any attention to what they say. They may indeed be excellent in their own way of thinking, but they have not yet reached enlightenment; and so we may say that the words of people who are trying to save themselves by their own efforts are very great hindrances to those seeking *Ōjō*. Let us not therefore adopt the methods of the unenlightened, but entrust ourselves to the Buddha's Vow and that only. The good father Zendō used to say, that we should not tolerate a single thought of doubt, on account of the opposition offered by those of another religious school to the Pure Land doctrine. It is better not to call in people of a different faith, but whoever they are, whether nuns or other ladies, tell her to have them always at her side repeating the *Nembutsu*. She should with one heart and mind lay aside all the religious counsel of the unenlightened, and trust only in the wise counsel of the Buddha."

(d) His Promise to Pray for Her

"The fact is that in my own case, the decision I made to shut myself up in my chamber for the *Nembutsu* practice is by no means intended for myself alone. And since I have heard of her illness, I shall direct all my prayers without exception toward the one object of promoting her *Ōjō*. So tell her that I am praying for her, that her deepest desires for *Ōjō* may be fulfilled.

How can it be otherwise than that this will be helpful to her, if indeed my own purpose in it be genuine? Believe me, it will surely be effectual. That she has listened with such attention to my words, shows a *karma* relationship extending beyond the limits of the present world, and is deeply rooted in a preexistent state. Now from what I hear, whether she precedes me into the other world or I unexpectedly precede her, there is no doubt whatever that we shall meet again at last in the same Pure Buddha Land. It matters not whether we meet again in this world, which is but a fleeting dream and vision. So let her not worry about that at all, but lay aside all such thoughts, and give every attention to the deepening and strengthening of her faith, and to the practice of the *Nembutsu*, and wait for the time when we shall meet in that Land. If she is now very weak, I am afraid that what I have said may be too long for her to take in fully, and in that case please just tell her the substance of what I have written. The news of her illness has stirred within me a strange sense of sorrow, which has impelled me to write." They say that she kept thinking of this letter as she went on repeating the *Nembutsu* up to the very last, till her longing for *Ōjō* was finally realized.

Awanosuke the Fortune Teller

A fortune-teller called Awanosuke, who was an attendant of Hōnen's, used to practice the *Nembutsu*. One day Hōnen called attention to this man's manner of doing it, and asked his disciple Shōkōbō, "Which do you think is the better, Awanosuke's way of saying it or Genkū's?" He, although in his heart quite understanding the purport of Hōnen's words, in order to confirm his own thought, replied, "How can it indeed be that your *Nembutsu* is always the same as his?" At this Hōnen, his cheeks highly coloring, said, "Well, to what purpose have you all along been listening to the doctrine of the Pure Land? That Awanosuke over there, when he asks the Buddha to save him, saying, '*Namu Amida Butsu*,' does just the same as I do when I offer that petition. There is not the slightest difference between us." Of course Shōkōbō had thought the same thing himself, but the heart and soul of the doctrine came to him as if for the first time, and the tears rolled down his face.

Kyō Amidabutsu, the Converted Robber

In the province of Kawachi, there lived a man called Shirō Amano, who was the chief of a robber band. He used to make a business of murdering people and stealing their goods, and thus passed most of his life. But after he had grown old, he came under Hōnen's influence and gave himself up to the religious life, being called by the name of Kyō Amidabutsu. After this he went to Hōnen and received instruction from him. Once in the middle of the night he thought Hōnen was wide awake, all by himself calling upon the sacred name. Kyō Amidabutsu coughed a little and Hōnen soon went to bed. From that time on, Hōnen seemed to be sleeping all through the night until the dawn. Kyō Amidabutsu thought it very strange, and yet he did not go so far as to call Hōnen and ask him about it. But somewhat later he went again, and found Hōnen in the chapel of the temple. He went up as far as the bare floor in front of the mats, and said to Hōnen, "I have no relatives in the city, so it will be hard for me to stay here much longer. I have a friend living in Kawamura in the province of Sagami, and I am intending to go and ask him to let me stay with him. As I am already an old man, it will be hard for me to come and see you again. Of course I am only an ignorant fellow, and so even though I was to be told all the deepest doctrines of the Law, it would be of little use to me, for I could not understand them. I should like just one word from you as to what one ought to do to make sure of his birth into the Pure Land, and I shall try to remember it all my life."

(a) Hōnen on the Meaning of a Sincere Heart

Then Hōnen spoke as follows: "First of all take note that there is nothing so extremely profound in the *Nembutsu* at all. The only thing is to know that everyone who calls upon the sacred name is certain to be born into the Pure Land. No matter how learned a scholar may be, he has no right to make out that there are things in our sect which do not belong to it. Do not by a great effort of your mind try to make yourself think that there is something so very subtle in the doctrine. As the calling upon the sacred name is such an easy religious exercise, there are many who practice it, but the reason why so few actually attain *Ōjō*, is that they are ignorant of this old well-known truth of the certainty of such birth to all who believe. Last month when you and I were here alone together, in the middle of the night, I got up and was practicing the *Nembutsu*. Did you hear me?" Kyō Amidabutsu replied, "I thought the sound of your voice in prayer struck my ears in my sleep." At this Hōnen went on to say, "This is the very *Nembutsu* that assuredly brings *Ōjō*. The *Nembutsu* of a hypocrite or of one practicing it for show does not lead to the Pure Land. The one who wants to make sure of it must not practice it for show, but with a sincere heart. A man does not act for show in the presence of little children or animals, but only before his friends and companions, or the members of his household who are always with him, his wife and children, if indeed the latter are old enough to know the difference between the east and west. The ordinary man who lives among his fellows is not without this heart of vanity. It matters not whether they be our intimates or strangers, nor whether they be high or low born, there is no greater enemy to our attainment of *Ōjō* than our fellow men. It is because of the presence of our fellows that vanity is awakened within our hearts, and so we fail to attain that birth after death. And yet however true that may be, none of us can live absolutely alone."

(b) Private Devotion

"How then is it possible to practice the *Nembutsu* with a heart sincere, and not with a heart which tries to do things that will please the eyes of men? One who is all the time living with other people, takes no time for quiet reflection, but is forever living a feigned life. Now if then, there is no one by to

Jōdo monk practicing the *Nembutsu*

see or hear him, he secretly rises from his couch in the middle of the night, and practices the *Nembutsu* a hundred or a thousand times to his heart's content, this is the kind of *Nembutsu* which is not practiced for show, but is in harmony with the mind of the Buddha, and of a certainty eventuates in birth into the Pure Land. So long as one practices it with a heart like this, it matters not whether it is done in the night-time or in the morning, at noon or at twilight. We must always do it as if no one were listening."

(c) Undistracted by Outward Things

"In short, what I mean by a heart that longs for certain birth into the Pure Land, and in all sincerity calls upon the sacred name, may be likened to the heart of a thief who is purposing to steal another's property. Down deep in his heart he means to steal, but as far as his outward appearance is concerned, he gives not the slightest indication to others of his purpose by look or gesture. As others know absolutely nothing about the purpose to steal that is in his heart, we may say that the purpose is for himself alone, without any reference whatever to outward appearances. Such an undivided heart as this is necessary in the man who would make sure of birth into the Pure Land. He must never for a moment allow himself to forget what he is about, by letting others know even by the slightest facial expression that he is calling upon the sacred name, even though he be in the midst of a crowd of people. At such a time, who but the Buddha should know anything about his practicing the *Nembutsu*? If only the Buddha knows, why have any doubts about birth into the Pure Land?"

(d) Two Types of Men

To this Kyō Amidabutsu replied, "I now quite perceive what the doctrine about certain birth into the Pure Land means, and fully understand it. If I had not heard your words of instruction, I might alas! have missed birth into the Pure Land at last. But it seems to me from what you have said that it is wrong to tell the beads of the rosary, or to move one's lips in prayer before men. Isn't that so?" Then Hōnen said, "No, you are mistaken on this point. The most important thing is to continue the practice of the *Nembutsu* without ceasing. This is why it is said you must always continually keep your mind on this one thing. To illustrate what I mean, we may say that there are two kinds of men in the world, the brave and the timid, though outwardly they all seem the same. The timid man, even when there is nothing at all to be troubled about, is frightened at the slightest appearance of anger in another man, and runs away and hides himself. The brave man, even when a fierce enemy appears, who really endangers his life, and he might help himself by running away and hiding, is not the least afraid, and does not shrink from him an inch."

(e) The True and the False

"In the same way there are the two kinds of men, the true and the false. With the false-hearted, it is natural to feign, and even when, for their own sake, the thing is so small that there is not the least need for it, they are sure to practice some deception. But on the other hand, the true-hearted, who speak no false word, even when it might be to their advantage to do a little feigning, take no thought for their own personal gain, but are true to the core, and feign not in the slightest degree. This is indeed their inborn disposition. Now if such true-hearted people desire birth into the Pure Land, and devote themselves to the *Nembutsu,* it matters not where they are, or in whose presence they practice it. Seeing that they do not feign in the least, their calling upon the sacred name is genuine and sincere, and is sure to issue in birth into the Pure Land. Why then should it be prohibited? Then again, even in the case also of a man who is false-hearted by nature, and does a few things insincerely, so as to appear well in the eyes of the world, if he comes in contact with a pious priest, and has a believing heart awakened in him, so that he forms a profound purpose to attain birth into the Pure Land, he makes up his mind to keep on repeating the sacred name without ceasing, and it does not matter where he is, or in the presence of what people, he just goes on repeating it with undiverted mind, and with all earnestness. This is a case of downright genuine *Nembutsu*, and such a man is sure of birth into the Pure Land. There is no need at all of forbidding him to practice the *Nembutsu* before others, if he does it in this way. What I have now said has reference to that one of the three mental states, the absence of any one of which, will, as Zendō has said, prevent one's being born into the Pure Land. I mean a sincere heart, which it is so particularly hard to have awakened within men, and that is the only reason why I have spoken as I have, so as to awaken it in you. This being the case, how could I indeed exhort you not to keep up the practice of the *Nembutsu* even at ordinary times from day to day?"

(f) How and When to Practice the Nembutsu

Then Kyō Amidabutsu asked him again, "When one practices the *Nembutsu* at night as you were saying, should he always get up out of bed and do it? And should he always have his rosary and sacred scarf on?" To this Hōnen replied, "The *Nembutsu* may be practiced whether one is walking, standing, sitting, or lying, and so it may be left with everyone, according to circumstances, to do it either reclining or sitting or in any way he chooses. And as to holding the rosary or putting on the sacred scarf, this too must be decided according to circumstances. The main point is not the outward manner at all, but the fixing of one's mind on the one thing, firmly determining to have *Ōjō*, and with all seriousness to call upon the sacred name. This is the all-important thing." At this Kyō Amidabutsu fairly danced for joy, and put his hands together in worship as he went away.

(g) The Robber's **Ōjō**

After this, when Hōrembō met Hōnen, he asked him if this had actually happened, and Hōnen said, "Yes, I heard he was an old robber, and I instructed him as I thought his case required. He seemed thoroughly to understand what I told him." So he went down to the village of Kawamura and lived there the rest of his life. When after a long illness, he was drawing near the end, he told his friend he was sure of birth into the Pure Land, and it was all due to his having believed what Hōnen had taught him. His last words were, "Go and tell Hōnen of my birth into the Pure Land," and without a single doubt, with his hands folded in prayer, he repeated the *Nembutsu* over some tens of times with a loud voice, and then passed away. So his friend went up to the capital and gave Hōnen a detailed account of his last days, at which Hōnen remarked, "Well, no doubt he did understand. This is fine."

Hōnen Shōnin

16. SAMURAI BELIEVERS

Tarō Tadatsuna In the province of Musashi there lived a samurai called Tarō Tadatsuna Amakasu, belonging to the Inomata clan, who was in the service of the Minamoto family, and he became a follower of Hōnen and very assiduous in the practice of the *Nembutsu*. Now at this time the priestly soldiers of the Enryakuji Temple were so unruly that, in defiance of the better element in the priesthood, they made a plot for an armed resistance against the authorities. They took their stand at the Hiyoshi Hachiōji shrine, and Tadatsuna was by Imperial order put in command of a body of troops which the Government dispatched thither to suppress the rising. As he was starting for the front on the fifteenth day in the eleventh month in the third year of Kenkyū (1192), he paid a visit to Hōnen and said to him, "I have often heard you say that even sinners like us, if they will only say the *Nembutsu*, and put their whole trust in Amida's Original Vow, will undoubtedly attain *Ōjō*. This has made a deep impression upon me, but I suppose it is the case only with those who are lying on a sick bed and calmly waiting for the end to come. But as for myself, being a samurai, I cannot do just as I would like, and now in obedience to an Imperial order, I am setting out for the castle at Hachiōji to chastise those obstreperous priests of Sammon. I was born in a soldier's family and trained in the use of the bow and arrow, being on the one hand under obligation not to fail in carrying out at least in some measure the will of my ancestors, and on the other responsible for handing down something of glory to my posterity. And yet if, as a soldier, I abandon myself to the driving back of the enemy, all sorts of wicked and furious passions are likely to be stirred within me, and it becomes very hard to awaken any pious feeling in my heart. If, indeed, I should allow myself to keep thinking all the time about the transitoriness of life, and trying not to forget the truth about attaining *Ōjō* by the *Nembutsu*, I should be in danger of being taken captive by my enemies, and thereby be eternally branded as a coward, straightway have all my patrimony confiscated, and so for a fool like me it is very hard to decide which of these courses to choose. Will you not tell me how I may accomplish my cherished desire for *Ōjō*, without on the other hand sacrificing the honor of my family as an archer?"

(a) His Ōjō *in Battle*

To this Hōnen made the following reply: "Amida's Original Vow says nothing about whether a man is good or bad, nor does it discuss whether a man's religious practices are many or few. It makes no discrimination between the pure and the impure, and takes no account of time, space, or any other diverse circumstances in men's lives. It matters not how a man dies. The wicked man, just as he is, will attain *Ōjō* if he calls on the sacred name. This is the wonderful thing about Amida's Original Vow. And so, though a man born in an archer's family goes to war, and loses his life, if he only repeats the sacred name and relies upon Amida's Original Vow, there is not the slightest doubt whatever that Amida will come to welcome him to His Paradise." Under these gentle instructions his doubts left him, and with a glad heart he exclaimed, "Tadatsuna's *Ōjō* will verily take place today." Hōnen handed him a sacred scarf which he put on under his armor, and he finally set out for the castle at Hachiōji, where he abandoned himself to battle with the rioters. In the midst of the struggle his sword was broken, and he received a deep wound. Seeing it was quite hopeless, he flung down his sword, and clasping his hands, with a loud voice he called upon the sacred name, and gave himself over into the hands of the enemy. Purple clouds covered the battlefield and many smelled the delicious perfume, and people said that purple clouds also hung over the northern mountain. When Hōnen heard about it, "Good," said he, "Amakasu has been born into the Pure Land."

Jirō Naozane At Kumagai in the province of Musashi there lived a warrior by the name of Jirō Naozane, who was in the service of the Minamoto family, and at the time of the great struggle with the Taira he distinguished himself in several engagements, so that he came to be regarded as second to none in soldierly qualities. It must surely have been from some inherited good in him that, when he grew discontented in his relation to his master the Shōgun (Yoritomo), his religious spirit was awakened, and he entered the priesthood, under the name of Rensei.[1]

[1] In those days men of the upper classes were in the habit of entering the priesthood. Although they did not entirely forsake their homes, still they put on priestly robes, practised religious exercises, sometimes in their own special chambers apart from their ordinary houses, and sometimes they changed their own houses into temples. From the Nara period of Buddhism down to Hōnen's day, the general conception of religion was that it was only by becoming a priest out and out that one could lead a perfect religious life. It was Shinran who was the first to oppose this clerical conception of religion, but the old ideas and customs continued dominant down to the middle of the Tokugawa period (1603-4867).

He called on Seikaku Hōin to ask some questions about matters relating to the future life, when he was told he had better ask Hōnen about them; so he went at once to see Hōnen in his humble thatched cottage. Whereupon Hōnen without a single word about his sins, whether they had been great or small, told him that the only thing he needed to attain *Ōjō* was to repeat the *Nembutsu*. On hearing that this was all he needed to do, he burst into such floods of tears that it startled Hōnen, but for a time he said nothing. Finally, Hōnen broke in with, "What makes you weep so?" At this he replied, "I supposed you would tell me I should have to cut off my hands and feet and give up my life if I would be saved, but instead of that you tell me the only thing I need to do to attain *Ōjō* is to say the *Nembutsu*. You make it so easy that I cannot contain myself for very joy. That is why I can't keep back the tears." Hōnen on seeing that he seemed to be in terror about his future lot, went on to tell him that the very purpose of the Original Vow was to provide *Ōjō* for ignorant sinners by the mere saying of the *Nembutsu*. And as he so fully explained the way of faith, Kumagai became an out-and-out *Nembutsu* devotee, entered Hōnen's service, and continued with him for a long time.

(a) Hōnen's Letter to Rensei

After his return to his own province he wrote asking Hōnen various questions on doubtful points, and Hōnen replied as follows: "I was very glad to receive your letter, as I had been wondering how you were since we last met. To come at once to the point, I shall confine myself to a few words about the *Nembutsu*. This *Nembutsu* practice is the only one prescribed in the Original Vow. Seeing that it says nothing about other practices, such as the keeping of the precepts, the reading of the Sūtras, reciting magical poems (*mantra*), meditation upon absolute truth, or the like, if anyone wants to be born into the Pure Land, let him make sure of practicing the *Nembutsu* required in the Original Vow, and then, if he wishes to do these other things over and above, all right. But the *Nembutsu* of the Original Vow is quite enough by itself. Zendō, who was himself an incarnation of Amida Buddha, said that the *Nembutsu* was the 'one fixed practice,' and so even filial piety is not part of the Original Vow, though in some circumstances one ought to practice it. Likewise with meditation upon the Sanskrit bronze letter, or the carrying of the pious pilgrim's staff, and such like,—none of them are required according to the Original Vow, and we need not bother ourselves about them at all. The picture representing the Amida Buddha coming down from the Pure Land to welcome his devotees should be worshipped with great reverence, but this is a quite secondary matter. The one thing to do is to repeat the *Nembutsu* over thirty or fifty or sixty thousand times a day, putting your whole heart into it, and then the result will be certain birth into the Pure Land. If you have any time to spare after saying the *Nembutsu*, then you may apply it to doing good works. The fact is, however, that if you put your whole heart into repeating it some sixty thousand times a day, what need will there be of doing anything else? If you say the *Nembutsu* over thirty or fifty thousand times, even if you should break a few of the commandments, that cannot affect your attainment of *Ōjō* at all. Only bear in mind that, even though the Original Vow does not call for filial piety, your mother is now eighty nine years old, and so this year at least you certainly ought to stay at home and help her as much as you can to find her way to the Pure Land. (Signed) Genkū, on the second of the fifth month."

Saburō Tamemori In the province of Musashi there was a vassal of the Minamoto family named Saburō Tamemori who was a samurai of Tsunoto. In the eighth month of the fourth year of Jijō (1180), Yoritomo, who was the head of the clan, fought with the men of the Taira clan at the battle of Ishibashiyama in the province of Sagami. Tamemori was eighteen years old at the time, and as he desired to take part in the battle, he hurried away from his home and joined Yoritomo. Later, he accompanied Yoritomo in his retreat over into the province of Awa, distinguishing himself in many ways as a loyal retainer. In the second month of the sixth year of Kenkū (1195), Yoritomo came up to the capital on his way to Nara, where he was to take part in the dedication of the new buildings of the great Tōdaiji Temple, and Tamemori went along with him, being at the time thirty three years of age. Arriving at Kyōto on the fourth day of the third month, he went to visit Hōnen in his humble quarters on the twenty first day of the month, and confessed the sins he had committed in various battles. Receiving instructions from Hōnen in regard to the principles of the *Nembutsu Ōjō*, he was not long in declaring himself a devotee of this sole and only practice, and after he had returned home, he was unremitting in his devotions.

(a) Tamemori's Wish to be a Priest

Thus under Hōnen's influence Tamemori became very zealous in his prayers for birth into the Land of Bliss. Thinking that, as he would be practicing the *Nembutsu* anyway, he might as well become a priest outright, but failing to obtain the Shōgun's consent, he asked Hōnen whether he could not, while still remaining a layman, be given a religious name, take upon him the vow of keeping the precepts, and also wear a priest's scarf (*kesa*). At this request Hōnen was much moved, and gave him a copy of a book written by Kwan-in, a Court ritualist, bearing upon the ten cardinal precepts, together with his own explanations of that concise account of the three ideals of conduct.[2] He also sent him the scarf he desired, and gave him Songwan as his religious name. On receiving such a reply from Hōnen, he went on with the *Nembutsu* practice just as if he had been a priest. A little later, when writing Hōnen, he asked him for one of his own rosaries. To this Hōnen replied somewhat as follows: "A request like this makes me feel as if it is not merely a matter of the present world, but of an intimate *karma* relation, we must have had in some previous life. So by all means make this the occasion for increased diligence in seeking the Land of Bliss. I now present you with this rosary, which I have been constantly using myself, and I hope you will be unremitting in your use of it and in calling upon the sacred name."

(b) Another Short Letter from Hōnen

In still another letter Hōnen sent him, occur the following words: "Now is the time to apply yourself to the attainment of *Ōjō*. Hard though it be to be born a man, that blessing has come to you. And hard though it be to come in contact with the teaching which explains to us about the *Nembutsu Ōjō*, that blessing too has been granted to you. A wholesome hatred of this present fleeting world, and a gearing for the Land of Bliss have been awakened in your heart. Deep indeed is the meaning of that Original Vow of Amida. It must be that you will attain *Ōjō*. So in the unshaken conviction that you will do so, be unremitting in your practice." Tamemori put all these into a brocade bag, which he always carried on his person, a very proper thing indeed to do.

(c) Songwan's Longing for Ōjō *Leads to His* Harakiri

In the first month of the seventh year of Kempō (1219), when the Shōgun Sanetomo died, Tamemori obtained official permission to become a priest, and so the name Songwan which Hōnen had given him was publicly recognized. After Hōnen's death, Songwan, as the years passed, longed more and more for Paradise, and his loathing of this present world kept deepening. He used to take out Hōnen's letters to read, when he would address himself to Hōnen's spirit, praying him to come and welcome him to the Land of Bliss.

[2] The three ideals of conduct include all duties for both priest and laymen—all human duty. 1) to observe all the precepts forbidding evil, 2) to practice whatever is good, 3) to benefit all sentient beings.

But several years passed without any answer. At last he called in Jōshōbō and a few other disciples of Hōnen on the twenty eighth of the tenth month in the third year of Ninji (1242), and asked them to conduct the *Nembutsu* service for three weeks as prescribed in the Sūtra. On the eighteenth day of the eleventh month, the last of the series, at the hour of midnight, while in the act of repeating the *Nembutsu* in a loud voice in the presence of Buddha's image, he committed *harakiri*, and with his own hands took out his entrails and wrapped them in his silk trousers, so that they might be secretly thrown into the river behind the temple. After doing this he turned to his associates and said to them, "Ever since I went into retirement as a priest, I pray every time for my late master (Shōgun Sanetomo) that he may be promoted in his rank in Paradise, so I cannot help longing to see him once again. Besides, Hōnen's words to me, 'be sure and meet me in Paradise,' keep ringing in my ears, and I cannot help feeling what a useless thing it is to go on living in a corrupt world like this, instead of being born into the Land of Bliss. Now the revered Shaka entered *Nirvāna* at the age of eighty, Hōnen attained *Ōjō* in his eightieth year, and I am now full eighty years old. The *Nembutsu Ōjō* is the eighteenth article in Amida's Original Vow, and today is the eighteenth day of the month. If I could attain *Ōjō* today just at the close of this our three weeks' *Nembutsu* service, that would be the thing above all else I most desire." Of those who gazed upon the scene resplendent with his burning zeal for birth into that Land, not a single one was tearless. He then put on the sacred scarf which Hōnen had given him, and, with his rosary in his hands, he turned himself towards the west, and sitting upright, with folded hands, he repeated the sacred name in a loud voice several hundred times, till precisely at the hour of the horse (noon), in the midst of his repetitions, he breathed his last. The sky was at once overcast with purple clouds, and sweet perfumes filled the chamber, and continued right up to the time of the cremation ceremony.

IV.

HŌNEN'S BIOGRAPHY: HIS FINAL YEARS

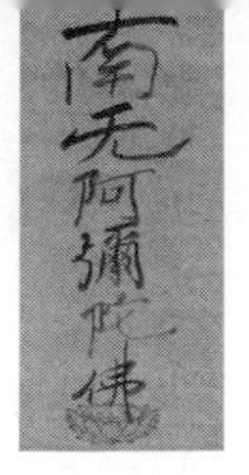

17. PERSECUTED ON ALL SIDES

The Beginning of Opposition The influence of Hōnen's teaching reached not only the Imperial Court, but extended as far as the sea-coasts on all four sides of the whole Empire. On the other hand, even among his own disciples, there were many who, on the pretext of observing the one and only practice of the *Nembutsu*, in reliance upon the Original Vow, were guilty of the most dissolute conduct, which became the occasion for the priests in the southern capital and in the northern mountain (Hiei) to devise means for abolishing the *Nembutsu* and hindering Hōnen's propaganda. In the reign of Tsuchimikado, it was rumored that there would be an uprising against Hōnen, on the ground that a teacher should be responsible for the faults of his disciples, but it all came to naught. However, in the winter of the first year of Genkyū (1204), the priests of all three sections of Mount Hiei gathered on the lawn of the grand Lecture Hall of the Sammon Temple, for the purpose of petitioning the Archbishop Shinshō to issue a prohibition against the sole practice of the *Nembutsu*.

The Hieizan priests' indignation meeting

Solemn Pledge of Hōnen and His Disciples

Hōnen on hearing of this, decided to quiet the resentment of the priests, and warn his disciples against the holding of distorted opinions. With this in view, he called his disciples together, and had over eighty of the foremost of them jointly sign a document in seven articles, which he had written as a solemn pledge and guarantee for future generations, and this he presented to the Archbishop. It ran as follows:

"To all my disciples and those priests who practice the *Nembutsu*, I make the following declaration:

1) You must not, in your devotion to Amida, through ignorance of the Sūtras and commentaries, adversely criticize the principles of either the Shingon or Tendai, or despise the other Buddhas and Bodhisattvas.

2) The ignorant must not get into angry disputes with men of profound knowledge, who differ from them in the theory and practice of religion.

3) You must not foolishly or narrow-mindedly insist on people of a different faith and practice from your own giving up their distinctive religious practices. Never jest at them.

4) You must not, in the name of the *Nembutsu* which you say requires no precepts, encourage people to indulge in meat eating, wine drinking, or impure sexual intercourse. Never say of people who strictly practice the religious discipline prescribed by their sect, that they belong to the so-called "miscellaneous practice people," nor that those who trust in the Buddha's Original Vow never need be afraid of sin.

5) Ignorant people, who are not yet clear in their own minds about moral distinctions, must not willfully press their own ideals upon others, departing from the sacred teachings of the Sūtras, and opposing the opinions of their teachers. You must not lead the ignorant astray by getting into quarrelsome disputes with them, which can only bring upon you the derision of the learned.

6) A dullard yourself, you must not undertake preaching about the way, and in ignorance about the righteous law, expounding all sorts of evil doctrines sure to influence for evil ignorant priests and laymen.

7) You must not set forth your own opinions contrary to the teaching of the Buddhas, wrongly calling them the views of your teachers.

Signed and sealed by the priest Genkū on the seventh day of the eleventh month of the first year of Genkyū (1204), the year of the rat and tree (*kinoe-ne*)."

Hōnen's Letter to the Archbishop Shinshō

In addition to the pledge above mentioned, Hōnen presented a letter to the Archbishop which was in substance as follows: "There is a rumor these days to the effect that Genkū is so devoted to the promulgation of the doctrines of the *Nembutsu*, that he runs down all others, with the result that all the other sects are declining, and the practices which they inculcate coming to naught. When I heard this report I was quite amazed. It seems that it has even reached the Sammon Temple, whose priests have said that I ought to be severely punished, and they have already presented a petition to Your Grace to that effect. Now on the one hand, I fear the punishments they may inflict upon me, while on the other I am grateful to them for their kindness. I tremble lest a man of such meager faith as mine is, should have incurred the displeasure of the Sammon priests as well as of the Court. But I rejoice because this will put a stop to the slandering of the Law of the Buddhas by my own disciples both in the city and in the country. If it were not for the warning I have thus received, how should I ever have been relieved of my anxiety about them? There is a passage in Amida's Original Vow which says, 'All will be admitted to my Land, except those who have committed the five deadly sins, and who have spoken evil of the Law of the Buddhas.' How can they who aim at the spread of the teaching of the *Nembutsu* be guilty of slandering the righteous Law? If anyone disseminates distorted views and empty lies, he deserves to be severely punished, in accordance with the strictest judgment, and I hope and trust that such will be so dealt with. Some time ago, when things of this sort occurred, I sent you a letter in which I went into all the particulars. And as the situation has not changed since then, it is hardly necessary to write again. But seeing that the evident purpose is to impose some heavy penalty for these supposed offences, I venture to address you again. There is no mistake in what I have said above. If I should be only making lame apologies with no basis in fact, I should utterly forfeit the benefit of my repetition of the *Nembutsu* seventy thousand times a day, should fall into and remain in the wretchedness of the three evil states after death, and indeed in this present world, as well as the

The enraged Kōfukuji priests

future, sink into intolerable torments, drinking for ages the deadly poison of perdition. On my bended knees I call upon all the holy Buddhas and Bodhisattvas in your august temple, and all the good deities who fill this mountain and extend their protection to the Law of the Buddhas, to bear witness to what I say. (Signed) Genkū, the seventh day of the eleventh month of the first year of Genkyū (1204)."

Hōnen's Warning Against the "Once Calling" Heretics

Hōnen also decided to issue a written instruction in prohibition of the "once calling" doctrine which runs as follow: "There are in these days a set of *Nembutsu* adherents who are both ignorant themselves and lead others astray. They have not yet come to understand the system of doctrine of our sect, and they are not even familiar with the technical terms of the Law. They are without devotion to the way. They are looking for their own personal advantage, and so with false words would they confuse men's minds with illusory thoughts. Thus are they planning for their own livelihood, with no thought of the punishment of their sin which awaits them in the world to come. As an excuse for their own do-nothing religion, they spread abroad in a most objectionable way the false principle of 'once calling,' and on top of that they start a new doctrine of no calling at all. Thus they lose the small merit of even the once calling. They cut off the little root of good they have, and further aggravate their sins already heinous enough. In order to indulge themselves in the momentary pleasures of the five lusts,[1] they do not shrink from the dreadful *karma* which will keep them in the three evil states throughout endless *kalpas*. They say, 'Ye who put your trust in the Amida's Vow need not be ashamed of committing the five deadly sins, and so go ahead and practice them to your heart's content. Do not wear the *kesa* (religious scarf), but put on the *hitatare* (ordinary clothes). Do not abstain from meat or from carnal passion. Eat as much as you like of venison or fowl', etc. Kōbō Daishi[2] used to say in reference to those who are in the lowest of all mental states, that they are like lambs and sheep which live only for food and sexual indulgence. Now these people surely belong to this degenerate class, do they not? They belong to the lowest of the ten mental stages in which men are found, and are destined to transmigrate through the so-called three evil states. Are not such indeed to be pitied? Not only are they opposed to the doctrines of all the other sects, but they have departed from the practice of the *Nembutsu* too. They encourage men in shameless idleness as to religious practice, and they would have the priests themselves cast away the commandments, and go back to the secular life entirely. We have never had such a heresy in our country before. This must be the work of devils. It means the destruction of the Law of the Buddhas and the perversion of the people."

The Heretical Suffer Punishment

But the ill-feeling of the priests of the Kōfukuji Temple did not cease, and at last they decided in the ninth month of the second year of Genkyū (1205) to present a memorial to the Government, demanding that Hōnen and his disciple Kintsugu, State Adviser of junior high rank, should be severely punished. So on this account an Imperial order was issued on the twenty ninth day of the twelfth month in the following terms: "For several years Genkū has been promoting the cult of the *Nembutsu* at large, both in the city and country, and many priests and laymen have been turning their attention to his instruction. But among his disciples there are some heretics, who, under the pretence of devoting themselves to this one religious discipline, have not

[1] The unlawful desires for carnal pleasures. There are two views held as to the meaning of these lusts. According to the first they are regarded as operating through the five senses. According to the other they mean passion for: 1) property, 2) the opposite sex, 3) eating and drinking, 4) fame, 5) sleep.

[2] Founder of the Shingon sect in Japan, lived 774-835.

hesitated to break the commandments of the Buddhas. Now this arises from the shallow-mindedness of the disciples themselves, who thereby are going contrary to Hōnen's original purpose. So the thing to do is to mete out strict punishment to these wrongdoers, but none to those who have been their instructors." As the number of *Nembutsu* believers at Court and among the people was by no means inconsiderable, only the heretical among his disciples were punished, and no penalty was imposed upon Hōnen.

18. HŌNEN SENTENCED TO EXILE

Anraku Beheaded

Thus the complaints which had been made against Hōnen by the priests of the southern capital and the northern mountain gradually subsided, and the *Nembutsu* cult went on its way without further interruption, until the following year, i.e. the first year of Ken-ei (1206), when, on the ninth day of the twelfth month, the retired Emperor Go-Toba happened to make a trip to the shrine on Mount Kumano. It so happened that at this time Jūren and Anraku and some other disciples of Hōnen were holding a special service for the practice of the *Nembutsu* at Shishigatani in Kyōto, in which they were chanting the hymns appointed for each of the six hours of the day and night. The chanting was so impressive and awe-inspiring, with its peculiar irregular intonation, that those who heard it were strangely swayed by mingled feelings of sorrow and joy, so that many were led into the life of faith. Among them there were two maids of honor to the ex-Emperor, who in his absence had gone to the service. On the Emperor's return from Kumano, it would appear as if some one told him about these ladies having become nuns, suggesting that there was something wrong about their relations with these priests, so that the Emperor was very angry with them, and on the ninth of the second month in the second year of Ken-ei (1207), he summoned them to the Court and imposed on them quite a severe penalty.

When Anraku heard the sentence, he recited the following passage from Zendō's *Hōjisan*: "When they see others engaged in their religious practices, they verily hate them, and, inspired by bitter enmity, they try by all means in their power to put a stop to it all. Infidels like this, born blind to the truth, who thus would destroy that practice which is the quickest and shortest road to salvation, shall themselves utterly perish, and even though they were to try to escape from those three states of misery ordained, and keep on trying for endless *kalpas*, they still would never be able to effect their escape." At this, the Emperor became more enraged than ever, and ordered Hideyoshi, one of his officials, to take Anraku out to Rokujō-gawara and put him to death. When he was saying goodbye to the officer in charge of the execution, he chanted the sunset hymn, when, to the great amazement of all beholders, purple clouds suddenly appeared in the sky. Whereupon Anraku turned to his executioner and said, "After I have repeated Amida's sacred name several hundred times, I shall then repeat it separately ten times. Just at the conclusion of the tenth, please let your stroke fall, and you will know that I have attained my long cherished desire for *Ōjō*, when you see me with my hands clasped, inclining to the right."[1] Thus saying he repeated the *Nembutsu* several hundred times, and then ten times at the end, when the executioner struck him. Everything happened just as he had said, as he fell to the right with his hands firmly clasped together. Many there were among the spectators, who, with tears of joy streaming down their cheeks, joined the cult of the *Nembutsu*.

Anraku's decapitation

Hōnen's Banishment to Tosa

Now through the influence of Hōnen's propaganda, multitudes of the wicked and ignorant who had been in the toils of the transmigratory round, came to believe and put their trust in that Original Vow of Amida. But it looks as if the king of the Māras[2] were thereby incited to still greater persecutions. For, after Anraku's execution, the Emperor's wrath continued unabated, the faults of the disciples being ascribed to their master, so that he was deprived of his priest's license, degraded to the rank of a layman, given the secular name of

[1] The historical Buddha, Shākyamuni, died while reclining on his right side.

[2] Demons.

Motohiko Fujii, and sentenced to banishment to a distant province.[3] It need hardly be said that the many who had looked up to Hōnen as their spiritual guide, high and low, priest and layman alike, whose hopes were set upon the attainment of *Ōjō* were overwhelmed with sorrow and grief no figure of speech can depict.

Hōnen Comforts His Disciples as He Leaves Them

As his disciples in his presence were lamenting their master's coming exile, Hōrembō said to him, "Jūren and Anraku have already suffered death as felons, but your banishment is wholly due to your propagation of the one and only *Nembutsu* way of salvation. Now you are old and decrepit, and I fear a stormy sea voyage to a distant land will endanger your life. Alas! that we can no longer look upon your gracious countenance nor listen to your lofty teaching. Would it not be a disgrace for us, your disciples, to stay behind and let you be taken into exile? Seeing that this is an Imperial edict, would it not be better for you now to say to His Majesty that you hereby give up the propaganda of the *Nembutsu* as the one and only way of salvation, yet secretly continuing it as you may be able, and thus possibly be released?"

To this counsel many of his disciples who were with him at this time gave their cordial consent. Then Hōnen said, "We must not resent this penalty of exile that has come upon me at all, for I am now an old man of eighty. Mountains and seas may divide us, but we are sure of meeting again in that Pure Land. Man is a being who goes on living when he grows weary of life, and is most likely to die when life is most dear. What difference does it make as to where we happen to be? But not only this, the fact is, I have labored here in the capital these many years for the spread of the *Nembutsu*, and so I have long wished to get away into the country to preach to those on field and plain, but the time never came for the fulfillment of my wish. Now, however, by the august favor of His Majesty, circumstances have combined to enable me to do so. Man may try to put a stop to the spread of this Law of the Buddhas, but it cannot be done. The vows which the many Buddhas have made to save men have come forth from their hearts' depths, and the unseen divine powers have conspired together to protect the Law against all opposition. Why then, should we have any anxiety over incurring the world's displeasure, and make that a ground for concealing from the public

[3] The idea of the sentence was that, as the priesthood was a sacred office, a priest as such could not be punished; so the first step was to deprive him of his priestly standing, and then administer punishment as if he were a layman.

the real import of the Sūtras and the commentaries which explain them? The only thing I am concerned about, is lest the gods who extend their constant protection over that Law of the Jōdo of which I, Genkū, am an exponent, should meet out punishment to those who of evil purpose thrust obstacles in the way of its propagation. For of all other ways of salvation known, this of the Jōdo is the most important, because it makes salvation certain, in these latter degenerate times, for all sentient beings. Let all those who outlive me take note that a fitting penalty will surely not fail to come upon all such offenders. If that law of affinity (*karma*) which operates in our mutual fellowship has not run its course, we may yet meet once more here in this present world."

Hōnen going into exile

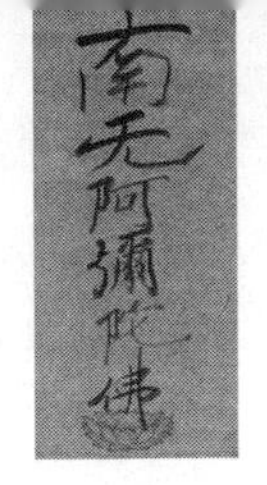

19. THE LONG LONELY JOURNEY

Hōnen Taking Leave of the Capital On the sixteenth day of the third month, when Hōnen left the flowery capital for the far distant province of his exile, Jō Amidabutsu, a samurai from Kakuhari, in the province of Shinano, who had charge of the men carrying the palanquin, as well as the sixty and more priests who accompanied them, thought that probably this would be their last journey with their revered teacher. Hōnen had never been accustomed to ride on horseback or in carriages or palanquins, but always wore straw sandals and went on foot. This time, however, he took a palanquin, because of his infirm age and the length of the journey. It was indeed a sorrowful leave-taking. I know not how many tens of thousands of all classes, high and low, gathered around him to say good-bye. The air was filled with voices of lamentation, and the tears of multitudes, lay and clerical, fairly watered the ground. Hōnen comforted them with such words as the following: "The holiest of men have always had to pass along the common highway. In China, for instance, we have the case of I-hsing (Japanese: Ichigyō) and in our own land of the sun, is the case of En no Ubasoku. In fact incarnations of the Enlightened One are quite in the habit of living in houses of exile. Other similar examples are found in the cases of the Chinaman Pai Lo-t'ien, and of our own countryman Sugawara, the well known Minister of State. Indeed everyone, whether living the life of illusion and passion, or transcending them, and entering into enlightenment, is like one dwelling in a house on fire. The man who has found reality, as well as the man who is still in the coils of the phenomenal, is like one traveling over a flooded road."

Poems of Farewell Now the ex-Regent Tsukinowa thought it too far from the capital to send Hōnen to the province of Tosa, and so changed his place of exile to Sanuki, his own domain. As a token of his inexpressible sorrow at parting, he sent Hōnen a letter with the following poem enclosed:

> Parting: a bridge that all must pass;
> To have you start, alas, alas!

To this Hōnen sent the following reply:

> What though our bodies, fragile as the dew,
> Melt here and there, resolved to nothingness?
> Our souls shall meet again, some happier day,
> In that same lotus-bed where now they grow.

Humble Converts at Takasago

When he reached the coast of Takasago, the province of Harima, many came with like purpose, among whom was an old couple, a man over seventy, and his wife over sixty years of age, who said to him, "We are fisher folk who live in these parts. From childhood it has been our business day and night to take the lives of fish for our living. Now as we are told that people who kill living things must go down to hell and suffer there, we want to know if there isn't some way of escaping this?" Thus saying, they folded their hands before him and wept. Hōnen looked pityingly upon them, spoke kindly to them, and said, "If you but repeat the '*Namu Amida Butsu*,' you will, by virtue of Amida's merciful Vow, be born into the Pure Land." On hearing this, they wept for very joy. Thereafter, though they continued their fishing by day, they kept repeating the sacred name all the time, and at nightfall on coming home, to the great astonishment of their neighbors, their voices could be heard all night saying the *Nembutsu*. Finally when they came to die, it

Hōnen teaching the fisherman at Takasago

was with much composure that they realized their longing for *Ōjō*. Hōnen afterwards hearing of it said, "This proves that anyone may attain *Ōjō* by practicing the *Nembutsu*."

The Harlot Converted When he arrived at Muro-no-tomari in the same province, a small boat drew near carrying a woman of ill-fame, who said to Hōnen, "I heard that this was your boat, and I have come to meet you. There are many ways of getting on in the world, but what sin could have been committed in a former life of mine, to bring me into such an evil life as this, which I seem fated to lead. What can a woman who carries a load of sin like mine do to escape, and be saved in the world to come?" Hōnen compassionately replied, "Your guilt in living such a life is surely great, and the penalty indeed incalculable. If you can find another means of livelihood, give this up at once, but if you cannot, or if you are not yet ready to sacrifice your very life for the true way, begin just as you are, and call on the sacred name; for it is for just such sinners as you, that Amida Nyorai made that wonderfully comprehensive Vow of His. So put your sole trust in it, without the least misgiving. If you rely upon His Original Vow and repeat the *Nembutsu*, your *Ōjō* is an absolute certainty." Thus kindly taught, the woman wept for joy, and later Hōnen said of her, "She is a woman of strong faith. She is sure to attain *Ōjō*." When afterwards he was on his way back to the capital, he called at this place and inquired about her. He found that from the time he had instructed her, she had retired to a village near the mountains in the neighborhood, and had been living there, devoting herself assiduously to the practice of the *Nembutsu*. A short time after, as death drew near, it was with great mental composure that she safely accomplished her *Ōjō*. On being told this, he said, "Yes, it is just as I had expected."

20. HŌNEN'S LIFE IN EXILE

Hōnen reaches his place of exile

Hōnen's Welcome to Sanuki

On the twenty sixth of the third month, Hōnen arrived at the residence of Sai-nin, a lay-monk formerly called Yasutō Takahashi, who was nominally the Vice-Governor of the province of Suruga, and Head of the district of Shiaku, in the province of Sanuki. This Sai-nin, the night before, had had a dream, in which he thought he saw the bright full moon coming into his sleeve, and while wondering what it could mean, Hōnen entered, and then he knew it must refer to Hōnen's coming. So he prepared a bath for him, and set delicious viands before him, and in every way possible provided him most hospitable entertainment. Hōnen, on his part, took great pains to explain to him the *Nembutsu* way of *Ōjō*, specially emphasizing the importance of strongly urging others to practice it, at whatever personal sacrifice. As an example, he cited the case of the Bodhisattva Sadāparibhūta, told of in the *Hokke Sūtra*, who patiently bore with the persecutions of those who spitefully threw sticks, tiles, or stones at him, when he was earnestly trying to bring all the four classes of men under the holy influence of the Law. As

Hōnen so strongly and impressively urged this upon him, saying, "This will benefit you more than the people you instruct," he replied, "I certainly shall do just as you say." Thenceforth he did nothing but practice the *Nembutsu*, for himself as well as for others.

Hōnen's Labors at Komatsu

The next place he stopped at was the village of Komatsu in the province of Sanuki. He lodged in a temple called Shōfukuji, where he dilated upon the uncertainty of all earthly things, and exhorted the people to practice the *Nembutsu*. Great crowds of men and women of every rank, from this and the neighboring provinces, gathered around him, much as they do in the market places, to listen to his teaching, and many of the vile and vicious mended their ways, while many others who had tried to find salvation by painful self-effort, gave it up as useless, and applied themselves to the *Nembutsu*, whereby they attained *Ōjō*. If we consider the great benefit the people of this distant province thus reaped, well may we say with Hōnen that his banishment was verily a gracious act of benevolence on the part of His Majesty. Up to this time there had been but one image of Amida as the main idol of this temple, but Hōnen during his sojourn here, had the usual two more added, constructing that of Seishi with his own hand.

Hōnen the Exile's Letter to Tamemori

The news of Hōnen's banishment spread far and wide, so that Tamemori Tsunoto in his distant province of Musashi heard it, and was so moved that he wrote to Hōnen in Sanuki, and received the following reply: "On the twenty first of the eighth month, I received your letter. I cannot tell you how deeply I appreciate your kind words, sent me from such a distant place. My present circumstances are my happy destiny, against which I have no word of complaint. Such is the common experience of human life, which I but share with my fellow men. We should anyway have a wholesome loathing of life itself, always ready to part with it on short notice, today or tomorrow, and so regard experiences like this as a matter of course, in such a foul world. Let us make sure of our *Ōjō*, and never dream of resenting what befalls us. Everything happens to us as a result of actions done in a preexistent state, and none of the evils of which the world is so full, has now appeared for the first time. So the thing for us to do is to make haste in ensuring our attainment of *Ōjō*." What a fine letter this is!

Hōnen's Visit to Kōbō's Temple During Hōnen's stay in Sanuki, he made it to all the sacred places in the province, among which was the Zentsūji Temple, founded by Kōbō Daishi in memory of his father. In an inscription on the temple, he found the words, "Everyone who pays a visit to this temple will be sure of having me for a companion in the Pure Land of the one Buddha." At this he was overjoyed and said, "Verily it was to see this that I was brought here."

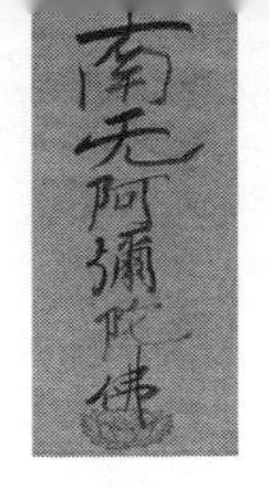

21. THE EMPEROR'S PARDON

The Decree of Release

Several of his court often used to try to persuade the retired Emperor to pardon Hōnen, but he was not yet so minded. It happened, however, that His Majesty had a strange dream, and besides this, Yorizane Nakayama, the Prime Minister, often remonstrated with him about it, greatly grieved as he was over Hōnen's banishment, for he could not get it out of his mind that Hōnen had been his father's religious adviser at the time of his death. "Can it be," he said, "that this *Nembutsu* cult is opposed to the mind of the Buddhas? I fear their anger may have been incurred, for our visiting a teacher with punishment for the faults of his disciples." Now it so happened that there was a dedication ceremony to celebrate the completion of the Saishō Shitennōin Temple, and the Emperor to signalize the event, granted a general amnesty to criminals. So in the same year, that is the first year of Jōgen (1207), on the eighth day of the twelfth month, Hōnen's pardon was granted, provided that he was not to be permitted to come back to the capital, but remain in the neighboring provinces.

Hōnen's Stay in Kachiodera

The news of the Emperor's pardon of Hōnen spread through the land, and his disciples in the capital were overjoyed at the thought of again meeting him, while the country people, where he had been, were grieved at the parting, so that his return from exile brought both joy and sorrow. On being released, he set out from the province of Sanuki, and on his way to the capital he came to a place called Kōbe in the province of Settsu, where he stopped for a time, and by his preaching brought great numbers of young and old of both sexes into the *Nembutsu* fold.

As he was not allowed to come to the capital, he stayed for a time in the Kachiodera Temple in Settsu, where the famous priests Zenchū and Zenzan had been carried up to heaven by angels, and the saint Shōnyo attained his birth into the Pure Land. In a valley in the temple precincts on the west, he had a small straw-thatched cottage built, and here he lived. It happened one day that he attended one of the ordinary services where the *Nembutsu* was being said with a peculiar musical intonation, and noticing how shabbily the priests were dressed, he sent Hōrembō, one of his disciples, to one of his believers in Kyōto to get fifteen suits of clothes made, which he gave to the priests of the temple. They were so glad and grateful for his kindness, that they held special *Nembutsu* services for seven days. This thatched cottage where Hōnen lived, remains to the present day, and is frequented by many visitors. It is said that there is a very delightful fragrance in the room he used to occupy.

Permission to Return to the Capital

Thus four years of retirement in the Kachiodera Temple passed, without his being allowed to return to the capital. It happened, however, that during the summer of the first year of Kenryaku (1211), the retired Emperor paid a visit to the Hachiman shrine, where he heard the sorceress in attendance say, "Heaven never shows partiality in the blessings or calamities it sends. Heaven is on the side of good men. A country is well or ill governed as its ruler is virtuous or otherwise. Alas! Alas! in these days our lord walks in the dark, his officials are crooked, the administration is corrupt, the people mourn. A terrible national revolution is at hand, and the country is threatened with devastation. There will surely be remorse of conscience for this." On the Emperor's return, his nearest retainers addressed him thus: "The oracle of the sorceress cannot be referring to any ordinary matter. Wickedness cannot vanquish virtue. Benevolence is the best way to banish vice, and a country cannot be governed better than by a virtuous administration. The way to get rid of wicked demons is to be devoted to the Laws of the Buddhas. Must you not then, to begin with remove the proscription of the *Nembutsu* practice, and grant full pardon to the priest Hōnen?"

And so on the seventeenth of the eleventh month of that year, Mitsuchika was dispatched as an Imperial messenger to announce to Hōnen that he might return, which he did on the twentieth of the same month. Everyone in the temple, in reverent regard for his virtue, grieved at his departure from the mist-covered countryside to the great capital, over whose Imperial palace the ninefold clouds[1] ever benignly hover. It was not long after his return, indeed only ten years,—before that violent revolution of the Jōkyū period broke out, and the whole country was in the utmost confusion, precisely as

[1] This expression probably owes its origin to the Chinese custom of surrounding the palace with nine successive walls, through whose gates one must pass to reach the innermost portal. This afforded a ninefold protection from the gaze of the common herd. The palace was further conceived as protected by the wings of nine heavenly cloud masses that hovered over the enclosure, thus enveloping royalty in the clouds of a sacred mystery.

the sorceress had predicted. When Hōnen's disciples were deeply mourning their master's coming exile, he had said to them: "The Pure Land way of salvation is essential for men in these latter corrupt days. The revered Shaka himself in his vow said that this one Sūtra about Amida would alone remain forever, and all the power of all the Buddhas is pledged to its protection, so that even though men attempt to stop the propagation of the Law, it never can be done. But what troubles me most is my fear lest the divine powers, which have conspired to protect the *Nembutsu*, should be angered at men's unreasoning hostility to it. The day is sure to come when people will know the truth of what I say."

His Welcome Home Accepting Jichin's invitation, Hōnen took his residence in a temple at Ōtani. We remember that in ancient times when our revered Shaka came down from the thirty-three-fold Heaven,[2] men, and *devas* vied with one another in their eagerness to be the first to see him. So after Hōnen had braved the waves of the southern sea, and come back to the capital, hosts of men and women crowded around him in glad welcome. It is said that a thousand or more visited him that first night, and, lonely place though it was, he had a constant stream of visitors daily.

The Emperor's messenger asks Hōnen to return to the Court again

[2] According to the *Mahāmāyā-sūtra* (vol. II), the Buddha, some years after his attainment of enlightenment, went up to this heaven, to return thanks to his mother Māyā, who had died seven days after his birth, and was thereafter born into this heaven. Shaka passed three months of the summer here, proclaiming the Law to his mother.

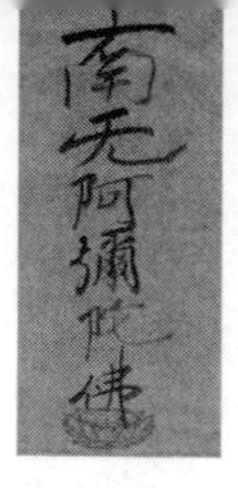

22. HŌNEN'S LAST HOURS

The End Approaching

From the second of the first month in the second year of Kenryaku (1212), Hōnen was so poorly for several days that he could hardly eat anything. For three or four years his sight and hearing had become so dull, that he could neither clearly distinguish color nor recognize voices. But now as the end approached, both senses became as keen as of yore, and everyone who saw him was filled with delight and surprise. On the second of the month he talked of nothing but birth into the Pure Land, repeating the sacred name without ceasing in a loud voice, and even in his sleep his lips continued to move. On the third of the month, one of his disciples said to him, "Do you think it means birth into the Pure Land this time for sure?" To which he replied, "I came from the Land of Bliss, and I am sure I am going back there." Then Hōrembō, another disciple, said to him, "All famous priests from ancient times have left memorial temples behind them, but none such has yet been built for you. Where then, shall we build yours?" His answer was, "If you erect a memorial to me over my grave, the influence of my teaching will be confined to one place, and not widely disseminated. But I assure you my memorial shall fill the land. The one purpose of my life has been the universal spread of

the *Nembutsu*. So wherever among high or low the *Nembutsu* cult is found, there is my memorial temple, though it be but in a thatched cottage of a humble fisherman."

His Vision of the Holy Ones

At the hour of the dragon (8 a.m.), on the eleventh of the month, Hōnen arose from his bed and in a loud voice repeated the *Nembutsu*. All who heard were moved to tears. He said to his disciples, "Repeat the *Nembutsu* in a loud voice. The Buddha Amida has come, and no man who repeats the sacred name can fail to be born into the Pure Land," and then, as of old, he proceeded to dilate upon the merits of the *Nembutsu*, saying, "The Bodhisattvas Kwannon and Seishi and many sainted beings have appeared to me. Don't you see them?" When they said, "No," he urged them all to greater earnestness in repeating the sacred name.

At the hour of the serpent (10 a.m.), on the same day, his disciples brought him an image of Amida three feet high, and, as they put it on the right side of his bed, asked him if he could see it. With his finger pointing to the sky, he said, "There is another Buddha here besides this one. Do you not see him?" Then he went on to say, "As a result of the merit of repeating the sacred name, I have, for over ten years past, continually been gazing upon the glory of the Pure Land, and the very forms of the Buddhas and Bodhisattvas, but I have kept it secret and said nothing about it. Now however, as I draw near the end, I disclose it to you." The disciples then took a piece of

Hōnen's vision of the three Immortals at his death

cord made of five-colored strands, fastened it to the hand of the Buddha's image, and told Hōnen to take hold of it. Declining, he said, "This is the ceremony for most men, but hardly necessary for me."

Happy Omens

At the hour of the serpent (10 a.m.), on the twentieth of the month, purple clouds were seen over the roof of his chamber, and, as the halo encircles the Buddha's head in art, there appeared in the midst of them a beautiful five-colored circular cloud, quite visible even to the crowds passing along the street. At sight of them his disciples told him, "There are purple clouds above you. Are you about to enter the Pure Land?" He replied, "This is grand! My birth into the Pure Land is for all sentient beings. These propitious omens are to help men to faith in the *Nembutsu*."

At the hour of the sheep (2 p.m.) of the same day, he looked up towards the sky five or six times without blinking, when his attendants, in surprise said, "Has the Buddha come?" "Yes, he has." At the hour of the horse (noon), on the twenty fourth, a great mass of purple clouds again appeared. Soon ten charcoal burners on the Mizuno-o peak of Nishiyama saw it, and came out and told his disciples, as did also a nun who saw it as she was coming down from the Kōryūji Temple. All who saw and heard were in raptures.

From the twenty third of the month, he had been incessant in his repetitions of the sacred name, calling it out in a loud voice for a half hour or an hour at a time. From the hour of the cock (6 p.m.), on the twenty fourth, right up to the hour of the serpent (10 a.m.), on the twenty-fifth without the least interruption, he continued with all his might in a loud voice calling upon Amida. Five or six of his disciples assisted him in turn, with their voices, until they became tired, but he, old and sick as he was, went right on—a thing indeed without parallel. All around him, priest and layman alike, were in tears.

He Dies in Peace

From the hour of the horse (noon) the same day, his voice began to grow weaker and weaker, only at intervals it became loud again. As he drew near to the end, he put on the nine-stripped sacred scarf (*kesa*),[1] the very one which had been handed down from Jikaku Daishi, and lay down with his head to north, and his

[1] Hōnen put it on because he belonged to the main line of priests, who had transmitted the "Perfect Precepts" originally promulgated by Dengyō Daishi.

Hōnen's death

face turned toward the west,[2] and recited the following passage from the Sūtra: "The light (of Amida) illumines all sentient beings throughout the ten quarters, who call upon the sacred name, protects them, and never forsakes them." With these words on his lips he breathed his last, as one falls asleep. After his voice was silent, his lips and tongue continued moving over ten times, while a bright smile overspread his features. His departure took place just in the middle of the hour of the horse (noon), on the twenty fifth day of the first month of the second year of Kenryaku (March 7, 1212). He was then in his eightieth year—the very age at which Shākyamuni himself died. Another strange thing was that it was in the year of the monkey and water, the very same calendar year as in which the world-honored Shaka had died. Is it not a most remarkable coincidence? With his death, went out the light of knowledge from the world, as once more the Buddha's sun sank from human sight behind the western horizon. Men of all classes alike mourned his death, as they would that of their own loved parents.

[2] This was the usual posture of Shaka in sleep, in which also he entered *Nirvāna*, and it became a rule for his disciples, in all subsequent ages; special warnings were given against other postures. With the head to the north, lying on the right cheek, one naturally looks westward. The lion, the king of beasts is said to sleep this way, and so did Shaka, the lord of men, and so should men, the lords of creation. Later with the Jōdo conception of the Western Paradise, this traditional westward attitude was regarded as specially fitting.

The Disciples Commemorate Him Contrary to His Dying Wishes

As Hōnen was drawing near the end, he gave the following dying charge to his disciples: "Build no memorial temple to me. If you want to show your feeling towards me, do it not by holding meetings in my honor, but let each show his gratitude for what I have done for him by practicing the *Nembutsu* privately. I fear that if you gather together in crowds, it may only result in strife and discord." Nevertheless, Hōrembō, following the usual custom, besides encouraging the individual practice of the *Nembutsu*, proposed the holding of memorial services every seventh day all through the seven weeks of mourning, and it was unanimously carried out.

Spread of the *Nembutsu* in Face of Imperial Edicts

After Hōnen's death, there were several occasions on which Imperial orders were issued for the prohibition of the *Nembutsu*, namely during the Kempō period (1213-1218), in the reign of the Emperor Juntoku; during the Jōō and Karoku periods (1222-1226), in the reign of the Emperor Go-Horikawa, and during the Tempuku (1233) and Yennō (1239) periods in the reign of the Emperor Shijō. But the rigor of such strict orders naturally became slackened, and it was hard to put a stop to the propagation of the cult, which, through the labors of Hōnen's disciples, spread

Hōnen's cremation

over the whole Empire, so that the voices of the *Nembutsu* believers could be heard far and near. In the *Larger Sūtra*, Shākyamuni says, "Even though all other religious practices should perish, the *Nembutsu* would continue for a hundred years beyond that." These are not mere empty words, for are they not in our own day finding increasing fulfillment in the happiness the *Nembutsu* is ever bringing to all classes?

Hōnen's Parting Message

As Hōnen was drawing to the end, Seikwambō said to him, "I have for many years been indebted to you for instruction and counsel in the way of faith in the *Nembutsu*. But now will you not write me something with your own hand, that you think will be good for me, that I may preserve it as a memento." At this he took up his pen and wrote as follows: "The method of final salvation that I have propounded is neither a sort of meditation, such as has been practiced by many scholars in China and Japan, nor is it a repetition of the Buddha's name by those who have studied and understood the deep meaning of it. It is nothing but the mere repetition of the '*Namu Amida Butsu*,' without a doubt of His mercy, whereby one may be born into the Land of Perfect Bliss. The mere repetition with firm faith includes all the practical details, such as the threefold preparation of mind and the four practical rules.[3] If I as an individual have any doctrine more profound than this, I should miss the mercy of the two Honorable Ones, Amida and Shaka, and be left out of the Vow of the Amida Buddha. Those who believe this, though they clearly understand all the teachings Shaka taught throughout his whole life, should behave themselves like simple-minded folk, who know not a single letter, or like ignorant nuns or monks whose faith is implicitly simple. Thus without pedantic airs, they should fervently practice the repetition of the name of Amida, and that alone."

The foregoing is without question Hōnen's autograph, and a truly worthy model for all men in these later degenerate times, and it is still in circulation, known as the *Ichimai Kishōmon*, "One-Sheet Document."

[3] The "threefold preparation of mind" refers to the three "mental states" described in Chapter 9 *intra*; the "four practical rules" as prescribed by Zendō are 1) treating with profound reverence and respect all sacred objects, 2) practicing nothing but the *Nembutsu*, 3) leaving no intervals of time between the *Nembutsu* repetitions, but keeping them up continuously, and 4) the continued practice throughout one's whole life of the foregoing three.

Hōnen's tomb at the Nison-in Temple in Saga

GLOSSARY

Amida Buddha—The Japanese term for the Buddha of Boundless Light (Sanskrit: Amitābha) and Boundless Life (Sanskrit: Amitāyus), who established the Western Paradise of the Pure Land. In Hōnen's religious worldview this Buddha is of primary importance, arguably of even greater importance than the historical Buddha, Shākyamuni. See also entry under Hōzō Biku.

Eight Sects—There were at the time of Hōnen eight officially recognized sects of Buddhism: 1) Kusha, 2) Jōjitsu, 3) Ritsu, 4) Hossō, 5) Sanron, 6) Kegon, 7) Tendai, 8) Shingon.

Hīnayāna (Lesser Vehicle)—One of the two great paths, or "vehicles" of Buddhism. Also known as the Southern School on account of its geographic distribution (generally South Asia). The term Hīnayāna is pejorative; those who practice this path use the term Theravāda ("Way of the Elders"). Of the two paths, Theravāda (Hīnayāna) is the more ancient. See also entry under Mahāyāna.

Holy Path (*Shōdō*)—Hōnen uses *Shōdō* (Holy Path) to refer to the forms of Buddhism that came before him and which do not recognize the centrality of Amida Buddha. According to Hōnen, the practice of the so-called Holy Path (*Shōdō*) properly belongs to an earlier, more perfect, period, when men were of superior capacity and wisdom. The practice of the so-called Pure Land (*Jōdo*) belongs to the current degenerate age, and offers a way by which those who are lacking in intelligence and virtue may attain salvation.

Hōzō Biku—The Japanese term for the Bodhisattva Dharmākara, who through practicing austerities for eons of time finally attained Enlightenment and became the Buddha Amida. See also entry under Amida Buddha.

Kalpa—A general term for a long period. The length of this period is so great that it cannot be defined by months or years. Buddhist scholars have invented such comparisons as the time it would take for a mountain of granite to be worn away by an angel flying over it once in a hundred years and touching it gently with its wings.

Karma—The law of affinity, or of moral causation. The idea that everything that happens to us now is the result of some former action.

Larger Sūtra—One of three central Sūtras of Pure Land thought. This Sūtra gives an account of the Bodhisattva Hōzō Biku's Vows and his fulfillment of them (see entries under Hōzō Biku and Original Vow). The so-called *Larger Sūtra* is labeled variously as: Sūtra of Adornment of the Realm of Bliss, Sūtra of Immeasurable Life, Sūtra of Infinite Life, etc.

Mahāyāna (Greater Vehicle)—One of the two great paths, or "vehicles" of Buddhism. Also known as the Northern School on account of its geographic distribution. Although there are many sects of Buddhism in Japan, they are all considered to be of the Mahāyāna school. The Mahāyāna (Greater Vehicle) contrasts itself to the Hīnayāna (Lesser Vehicle). See also entry under Hīnayāna (Lesser Vehicle).

Meditation Sūtra—One of three central Sūtras of Pure Land thought. This Sūtra describes the recitation of Amida's name (the *Nembutsu*) as a way of obtaining birth into the Pure Land. Zendō's commentary on this Sūtra was a primary influence on Hōnen. See also entries under Zendō and *Nembutsu*.

Nembutsu—The practice of calling upon Amida Buddha's sacred name through the repetition of the phrase, "*Namu Amida Butsu*" (I take refuge in the Buddha Amida).

Ōjō—Birth into Amida's Pure Land, at the moment of one's bodily death. Purple clouds and a sweet smell often accompany a believer's *Ōjō*.

Original Vow—Before he attained perfect Enlightenment and became the Buddha Amida, the Bodhisattva Hōzō Biku made Forty-eight Vows (collectively known as the Original Vow), including the all-important vow that he would accept Enlightenment only on condition that each person who calls upon his name with faith but ten times, or even once, shall be born into his Pure Land of Bliss. See also entries under Hōzō Biku and Amida Buddha.

Other-Power (*Tariki*)—The reliance on the power of another (Amida Buddha) to bring about one's salvation. For contrast, see entry under Self-Power (*Jiriki*). For related concept, see entry under Three Periods of the Law.

Precepts (*Śila*)—Members of the priesthood must recite and swear to follow the ten "Perfect Precepts," or the "Commandments", namely 1) not to kill, 2) not to steal, 3) not to commit adultery, 4) not to lie, 5) not to exaggerate, 6) not to slander, 7) not to be double-tongued, 8) not to covet, 9) not to be angry, 10) not to be heretical. Non-priests may also dedicate themselves to following the Precepts. A priest must "administer" the Precepts to the person who "receives" them.

Pure Land (Jōdo)—The Paradise of Amida Buddha, into which are born those who call with faith upon Amida's sacred name. Amida's Pure Land of Bliss is a stage on the path to total Enlightenment; once born there one is certain of ever progressing, morally and intellectually, until attaining to perfect Enlightenment.

Self-Power (*Jiriki*)—The view that one can attain salvation by means of personal effort. Hōnen rejects *Jiriki* in favor of *Tariki* ("Other-Power"). See also entry under Other-Power (*Tariki*).

Shaka—The Japanese term for the Buddha Shākyamuni, the historical founder of Buddhism.

Three Evil States—The three evil states are hell, the realm of hungry ghosts, and animality, which can be interpreted also as states of mind.

Three Periods of the Law—A theory of the progressive degeneration of Buddhism after the passing of the historical Buddha, from the period of the perfect Law, to the imitation of the Law, to the ending of the Law. We live in the latter degenerate days of *mappō*, the final period during which time the only suitable religious practice is the *Nembutsu*. See also entry under *Nembutsu*.

Zendō—A Chinese Pure Land scholar (613-681). Hōnen's most significant intellectual and spiritual influence, considered by him to be an incarnation of the Bodhisattva Seishi, or even of Amida Buddha. Called Shan-tao in Chinese.

INDEX OF SIGNIFICANT FOREIGN TERMS

For a glossary of all key foreign words used in books published by World Wisdom, including metaphysical terms in English, consult:www.DictionaryofSpiritualTerms.org.

This on-line Dictionary of Spiritual Terms provides extensive definitions, examples and related terms in other languages.

BIOGRAPHICAL NOTES

JOSEPH A. FITZGERALD studied Comparative Religion at Indiana University, where he also earned a Doctor of Jurisprudence degree. He is a senior editor at World Wisdom and a professional writer. For twenty years, Joseph has traveled extensively throughout the Buddhist world, including visits to Bhutan, Mongolia, Cambodia, Burma, Thailand, Indonesia, Nepal, and India, as well as three trips to Japan. He is currently editing several forthcoming books on traditional spirituality. He lives with his wife in Bloomington, Indiana.

CLARK STRAND is the author of *Seeds from a Birch Tree: Writing Haiku and the Spiritual Journey* and *Meditation Without Gurus: A Guide to the Heart of Practice.* A former senior editor of *Tricycle: The Buddhist Review* and a respected authority on contemporary Buddhist practice in the West, he has written and lectured widely on Pure Land Buddhism.

ALFRED BLOOM, Professor Emeritus, University of Hawaii, was the first Proctor of the Center for the Study of World Religions at Harvard University. He received his Ph.D. from Harvard University, and taught World Religions and Buddhism at the University of Oregon and the University of Hawaii. He was Dean at the Institute of Buddhist Studies, Berkeley, sponsored by the Buddhist Churches of America, and is an ordained Shin Buddhist priest. His publications include: *Shinran's Gospel of Pure Grace*; *Shoshinge: The Heart of Shin Buddhism*; *Strategies for Modern Living: A Commentary with Text of the Tannisho*; *The Life of Shinran Shonin: The Journey to Self Acceptance*; and *The Promise of Boundless Compassion: Shin Buddhism for Today.*

HARPER HAVELOCK COATES first came to Japan in 1890, where he was a missionary of the Canadian Methodist Church, and a professor of New Testament Exegesis and Theology, Aoyama Gakuin, Tōkyō. **RYUGAKU ISHIZUKA** was born in Japan, where he was a priest of the Jōdo sect, and a professor of Buddhist Ethics, Shunkyo Daigaku, Tōkyō. Both men devoted over fifteen years of their lives to the translation of *Honen the Buddhist Saint: His Life and Teaching*, published in 1925.

Other Titles on Buddhism by World Wisdom

The Buddha Eye: An Anthology of the Kyoto School and Its Contemporaries
edited by Frederick Franck, 2004

A Buddhist Spectrum: Contributions to Buddhist-Christian Dialogue
by Marco Pallis, 2004

The Essentials of Shinran: The Path of True Entrusting
edited by Alfred Bloom, 2007

The Golden Age of Zen: Zen Masters of the T'ang Dynasty
by John C.H. Wu, 2004

Honen the Buddhist Saint: Essential Writings and Official Biography
edited by Joseph A. Fitzgerald, 2006

The Laughing Buddha of Tofukuji: The Life of Zen Master Keido Fukushima
by Ishwar Harris, 2004

Living in Amida's Universal Vow: Essays in Shin Buddhism
edited by Alfred Bloom, 2004

Naturalness: A Classic of Shin Buddhism
by Kenryo Kanamatsu, 2002

Samdhong Rinpoche: Uncompromising Truth for a Compromised World: Tibetan Buddhism and Today's World
edited by Donovan Roebert, 2006

Treasures of Buddhism
by Frithjof Schuon, 1993

The Way and the Mountain
by Marco Pallis, 2008

Zen Buddhism: A History, Vol. 1: India and China
by Heinrich Dumoulin, 2005

Zen Buddhism: A History, Vol. 2: Japan
by Heinrich Dumoulin, 2005